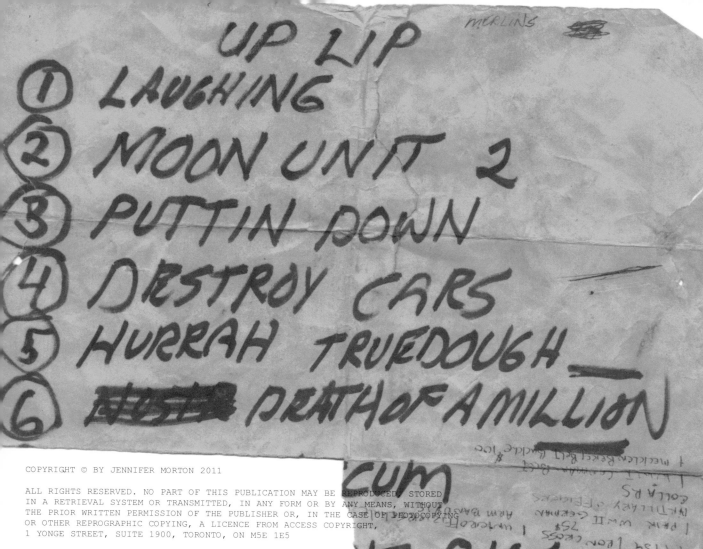

UP LIP

① LAUGHING
② MOON UNIT 2
③ PUTTIN DOWN
④ DESTROY CARS
⑤ HURRAH TRUEDOUGH
⑥ ~~NOISE~~ DEATH of A MILLION

LIBRARY AND ARCHIVES CANADA CATALOGUING IN PUBLICATION

MORTON, JENNIFER, 1962-
DIRTY, DRUNK AND PUNK : THE TWISTED CRAZY STORY OF THE BUNCHOFUCKINGOOFS
/ JENNIFER MORTON.

ISBN 978-1-897415-28-3

1. BUNCHOFUCKINGOOFS (MUSICAL GROUP). 2. ROCK GROUPS--CANADA.
3. PUNK ROCK MUSIC--CANADA. I. TITLE.

ML421.B942M88 2011   782.421660922   C2011-900319-8

THE PUBLISHER GRATEFULLY ACKNOWLEDGES THE SUPPORT OF THE CANADA COUNCIL,
THE ONTARIO ARTS COUNCIL, AND THE DEPARTMENT OF CANADIAN HERITAGE THROUGH
THE BOOK PUBLISHING INDUSTRY DEVELOPMENT PROGRAM.

BOOK DESIGN: BILL DOUGLAS

PRINTED AND BOUND IN CANADA

INSOMNIAC PRESS
520 PRINCESS AVENUE,
LONDON, ONTARIO, CANADA, N6B 2B8
WWW.INSOMNIACPRESS.COM

BUNCHOFUCKINGOOFS
BUNCHOFUCKINGOOFS
BUNCHOFUCKINGOOFS
BUNCHOFUCKINGOOFS
BUNCHOFUCKINGOOFS
BUNCHOFUCKING
BUNCHOFUCK
BUNCH

six

RESPOND TO A THREAT
WHEN NO ONE GETS HIT
BUT WHEN THE SHOTS DON'T STOP
SOMEONE TAKES THE SHIT
NOT WANTING TO PLAY
BUT PUT ON THE SPOT
THE 2 KIDS RETALIATE
AND LAND THE FIRST REAL SHOT
ONLY TO STOP POT ASTOP
THREATS TO THE TIME WASTING
A FEW HEADS GET BUSTED
NOW HATE YOUR REGRETS
NOT ABLE TO DEAL
WITH IT BY YOUR SELVES
YOU START A CONSPIRCY
COS YOU NEED SOME HELP
GETTING PEOPLE INVOLVED
UNDER FALSE PRETENCE

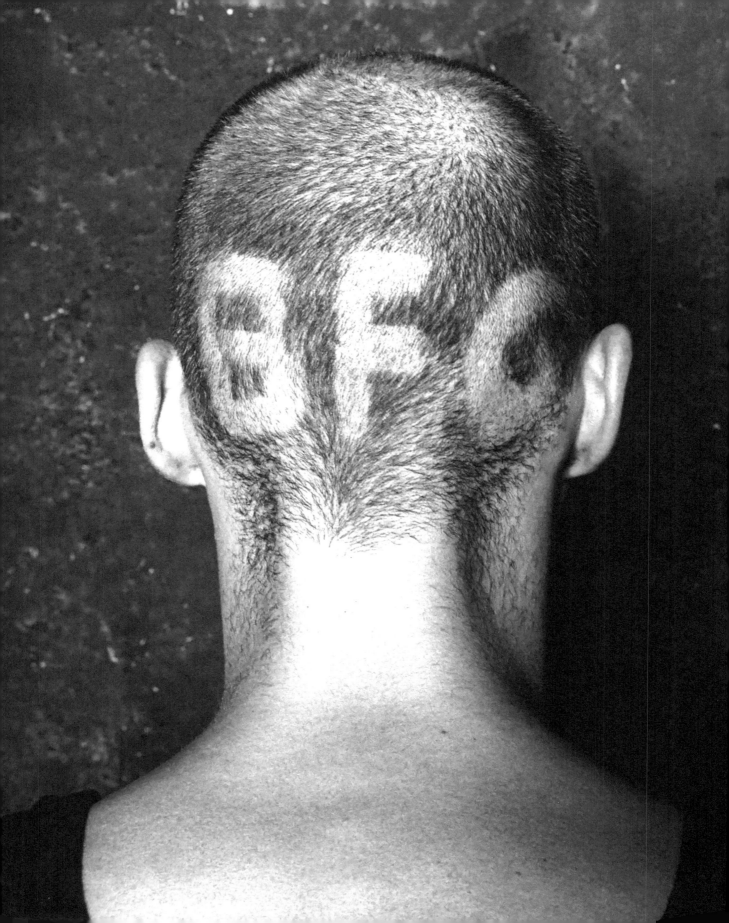

DIRTY, DRUNK AND PUNK

THE CRAZY TWISTED STORY
OF THE BUNCHOFUCKINGOOFS

Jennifer Morton

and Kisha Ferguson

Design by Bill Douglas

INSOMNIAC PRESS

"WE WERE A BUNCH OF DRUGGED OUT, DRUNKEN FUCK-UPS BUT WE MANAGED TO HAVE A DIRECTION AS OPPOSED TO FULL ON CRASH AND BURN."

CRAZY STEVE GOOF

DIRTY, DRUNK **AND** PUNK

GOOF STYLE

They were a bicycle gang, an art collective, a hard-drinking, fist-swinging punk rock band, and a family. And in 25 years of angry existence, they even turned into a political force: a cult of angst-ridden idealists whose lifestyle and philosophy epitomized D.I.Y.

They were anti-establishment, anti-consumerism, anti-car, and true to Punk style, anti-cop. They were hardcore with hearts. They drank too much and fought even more. They made their own music, their own clothes, posters and recordings, and lived commune-style at Fort Goof.

Their name even made it onto the Berlin Wall.

The Bunchofuckingoofs were born on a dare in 1983 when they were asked to open for Punk band United State at Larry's Hideaway in Toronto. Lead singer Crazy Steve figured "...we better call ourselves a bunch of fucking goofs before anyone else does."

Crazy Steve Goof was also the gang leader and den father to a motley crew of misfits, twenty-five of whom actually played in the band — as well as an assemblage of satellite fans and hangers-on. They included Thor, Mike Anus, Bambi, Katy, Scumbag, Mucus, Citizen Greg, MadDog, King Kong, Godzilla, Bones, Fetus, Stompin' Al, Airock, Fisty the Clown, Greenie and Goose. Given names were about as cool to the Goofs as soft, AM radio rock.

They lived outside of society and within one of their own. A society where dogs ruled, beer was currency and no one made plans beyond the next gig. The Goofs were made up of outcasts: street kids, kids from the burbs who didn't fit in, runaways and those who didn't or just couldn't conform to mainstream society. United in anger, they gave the finger to homogeneity and lived as they saw fit, in anarchy and chaos. Still there were rules, an unwritten Punk code that said no to needles, sniffing glue, panhandling, stealing, hitting women or sleeping with other people's girls [Rule #5]. Do any of these things, and you got your head kicked in. Lots of heads got kicked in. And they never called the cops [Rule #5]. If trouble broke out in their neighbourhood, they dealt with it in Goof style.

They were the kings and queens of Kensington Market, a four-block, multicultural enclave in the heart of Toronto, right next door to the city's never sleeping Chinatown. Here, among the fruit and vegetable sellers, fishmongers, butchers, roti shops, used clothing stores and counterculture aesthetic, they set up a series of Fort Goofs. The Goofs lived here knowing they wouldn't be harassed for their looks or their lifestyle. They returned the favour by taking care of their backyard: keeping drugs and Skinheads out of the Market, and earning the respect of others who also called it home.

Now to the music... It was angry, choppy poetry puked through a mic. Part of the second wave of Punk, it was a reaction to one of the most conservative decades in history, when greed was seen as good, the threat of nuclear annihilation constant and the idea that you could die tomorrow made you want to party today.

Live shows were Punk performance art in road warrior gear: what Spin magazine described as a "gnashing brand of apocalyptic abuse metal." As the spit flew from the angry mouth of Steve Goof, TVs got smashed, bottles thrown, faces cut, bones broken; the audiences came for the spectacle as much as the music. The Goofs never played covers and never sold out. After all it wasn't about the money...there's no money in being Punk. It was all about Punk pride.

They were out of control and so was their music. The BFGs made at least five recordings including *Carnival of Chaos and Carnage* and

There's No Solution So There's No Problem. They opened almost every show with "Alcoholiday Turned Alcoholocaust" – a song about drinking too much – and closed with "Pre-Programmed" – a rant about being brainwashed by TV.

And the craziness didn't stop at the shows. There were other Punk houses in Toronto but none as legendary as the Forts. They were booze cans open twenty-four hours a day, seven days a week, that sometimes stunk like rotten meat, and were also where the Goofs lived. They slept in cages, built to keep the drunks out and the dogs in. Inside this Punk bunker they jammed, printed band t-shirts and posters, gave each other tattoos and recorded music. A Punk version of Andy Warhol's Factory, furnished with whatever could be salvaged or found on the street, including people who needed a place to crash for the night.

William Burroughs said, "I always thought a Punk was someone who took it up the ass." So what the fuck is Punk? If Punk means banding together, rejecting mainstream society and saying, "fuck you" to the world, then the BFGs are Punk. Of course, they don't give a fuck what you think they are, and they'll be the first to tell you.

Some of the stories in Dirty, Drunk and Punk are recalled from beer-addled brains, remembered through the haze of time or passed down through a kind of oral broken telephone. If you have a problem with something someone said, take it up with the person who said it, not me. There's been enough ass kicking in the twenty-five years the Goofs have been around, leave mine alone.

Cheers,

JENNIFER MORTON

Bottom photo, opposite page: Godzilla, MadDog, Scumbag, Crazy Steve Goof

This book
is dedicated to
Skinheads, Glueheads
and Cops.

Berlin Wall, West Germany, 1989

BIRTH OF THE GOOFS

The party started before the band. Living together as Punks, selling beer and hanging in the downtown underground was the start. Back in the day, before the Bunchofuckingoofs were a band, there was the Back Alley Boys. The BABs were a bike gang, lead by Pil (his original name was Paul L.) "This is before Johnny Rotten, and Public Image," notes Vic Notorious, an original BAB. (Pil died of AIDS from sharing needles.) The other original BABs were Crazy Steve, Reverend Brown, Marky Thud, Scrag, Furball, Biff, Tynk and Vic Notorious.

The BABs were identified by a British American Petroleum patch. When the company went out of business, the boys scored dozens of patches. It happened around the time the Goofs formed. They sewed the B/A patch on their jackets, rode the alleys to avoid cops and banded together in the Baldwin Fort.

All they needed was a bike and a beer. Dressed like trouble, they took the alleyways as a way of avoiding cops and other enemies. Hassle free. They didn't stray far from the Fort. Bikes represented freedom, unlike cars that pollute and cost money, which means you need to work for the man and play by the rules.

"We don't ride like normal people. We ride like nine-year-olds. We crash at every opportunity," notes Crazy Steve Goof.

While most Toronto two-wheelers were riding skinny-wheeled ten-speeds, the BABs favoured old pedal-brake bikes, painted matte black, with fat tires and motorcycle-style handlebars. Oh yeah, and they all had girl frames, meaning no crossbar to get in your way when you had to ditch them in a hurry if the heat was on or throw them to the ground before a fight. The bikes were cheap and disposable, and easily thrown down stairs, over fences or at someone. And if they were ditched and not there the next day, no problem. Another one cost around thirty bucks, if one couldn't be found in the garbage and fixed.

The Back Alley Boys spent many long nights on acid biking around the abandoned Massey Ferguson buildings in the area south of King Street West now known as Liberty Village. The thousands and thousands of heated square feet were connected by ramps and hallways. There was even a "lake" in the bottom of the warehouse at 9 Hanna Avenue.

One night they found a few boxes of the union pins worn by workers. They were thick, hard, silver metal squares with Massey Ferguson stamped on the top, and Toronto Works proudly embossed underneath — solid. The Massey Ferguson pin was more or less another identification of being a Back Alley Boy, that later became the ID for the BFGs. Micus described it as a square sheriff's badge.

It meant a lot to have a pin. It wasn't an initiation. You had to be around, part of the scene, help out, understand the lifestyle and play by the Goof code. It was an honour to have Crazy Steve reach into the box and pass one over. They all still have their pins today. A few of the pins belong to girls.

"You weren't actually part of the Goof scene unless you had this Massey Ferguson pin on your leather jacket," says Susana. "It wasn't a big loud thing that proclaimed you were part of something. So you had to kind of know what it meant. It wasn't something given out to everybody who passed through the door, and I'd been around for a while and got to know a lot of those people really well."

"If the shit was hitting the fan and we were in a public place, you'd just flip it upside down," says Micus. "If I walked by you and you saw my pin was upside down, you'd instantly go into alert, be on your toes and flip your pin upside down."

Around the same time, Steve, in a drunken stupor agreed to open for the band United State. It was a dare that he immediately forgot. Once reminded, he and Scrag needed to come up with a band and a name in a week. The name kept going through different changes — first it was Back Alley Boys. Gang Green was one option, but another band had it. They thought about calling themselves The Oppressed, but it somehow didn't fit. Figuring they would suck, they decided to call themselves The Bunchofuckingoofs. Figuring that everyone else would call them that anyway.

"In jail slang, calling someone a goof means you want to fight," says Crazy Steve Goof. "If someone doesn't start swinging as soon as they hear the word, they are considered a pussy, and whatever shit is going on, is guaranteed to get shittier."

"I always thought that one of the bravest things about those guys is the fact that they called themselves Goofs," says William New. "It's an incredibly brave and odd Punk notion. I think that 'goof' is strictly a Canadian thing. I don't think if you went to America, in jail, and called someone a goof it would create quite the same firestorm."

The BABs became the Goofs. The Fort became Fort Goof, the band rehearsal space, recording studio and sleeping quarters.

MadDog had a terrible motorcycle accident while working as a manager at a retail sports store. Workers Compensation kindly funded the band's first drum set and also a great guitar that Bambi ended up snagging.

Four days before their first show they wrote seven songs.

Like true artists, they wrote about what they know. "Black Russians rule — fuck blow, Bang down a two-four — let the piss flow." That's their first song, "Alchoholiday Turnded Alchoholicaust." They ended up singing it at pretty much every show and it appears on every recording.

The first show had to be full-frontal Goof attitude. They showed up at Larry's Hideaway on bikes, stoned on mushrooms, and blasted off eight tunes. Crazy Steve's dog, Dirt, and Scrag's dog, Slag, ended up on stage too.

"Alcoholiday opened the set, and the crowd's fucking freaked," says John Tard. "Steve is looking at everybody in the eye, screaming 'We're BFG, I am BFG, I believe BFG, fucking watch this shit.'"

"We acted like total fucking idiots, told everybody to all go fuck off, fucking see you later and goodbye," says MadDog. "We figured it was the only show we were ever going to do."

MadDog, Scrag, Bambi and Crazy Steve Goof made up the original Goofs. Crazy Steve Goof hit the stage wearing an army helmet, with his face painted with an army camo stick, wearing a red pair of long underwear, chain belt, leather jacket and combat boots. Bambi made a BFG t-shirt, dyed her hair red to match, sewed together plaid pants and threw a chain over her shoulder.

Director Edward Mowbray, who was shooting a documentary about the hardcore music scene in Toronto called *Not Dead Yet*, captured that first show on film. Steve rants into the camera "Welcome to 1984…I am ready for the third world war…even if it starts in my own backyard."

Walking to the Scott Mission on Spadina for breakfast Mowbray has his camera rolling. They look like a young pack of misfits — guys and girls experimenting with living outside the box. Crazy Steve Goof tries to explain. "They is them. Them is a generalization, of anyone who isn't us; we are us,

they are them. Fuck them, don't fuck with us."

"They were fucking Punks, they wanted to present an image," says Mopa Dean. "The dogs were on stage, the bikes were all there….it was more about an attitude and an event than actually being a band and playing music."

"I watched Steve Goof on stage and I thought to myself that he makes it look easy," say John Tard. "Not to suck Steve's dick because, let's face it, I've seen a million front men, but he commanded the crowd. I always judge a singer by one thing…does he sing with his eyes open?"

The band's first recording, *There Is No Problem, So There's No Solution*, a double single, got made after Crazy Steve Goof bought a hundred Valiums because he wanted to stop drinking. Problem was, he'd take the Valium, have a beer, forget he wasn't drinking and then forget he was taking Valium. Over the next month he'd score 1000, sell 300 and take the rest. When he 'woke up', he was a wreck. Everybody was pissed because he'd become like a crazed dictator.

The BFGs were born and then began to multiply. They became an institution, a term they hate as much as 'gang' and yet both apply. Mentioning them in Toronto is a kind of test…true downtowners knew them, or had heard about them, and the most unexpected people oddly enough have a story to tell about them.

Some of the stories in this book are true and some might not be. Some are embellished and some have been left out of these pages entirely.

Crazy Steve Goof, MadDog, Scrag, Bambi. The Original BFGs

021

LARRY'S HIDEAWAY
121 CARLTON AT JARVIS
IN TORONTO

BFG BFG
UNITED STATES
FUCKING

GUARANTEED SEATING TILL 8:00 PM
NO REFUNDS OR EXCHANGES
ADMIT ONE • PROOF OF AGE REQUIRED

ADMIT ONE THIS DATE ONLY

NO REFUND PRICE NO EXCHANGE

LARRY'S
HIDEAWAY

$3.00

SEC   ROW   SEAT

GEN. ADM.

2996

"I SAW THEM THE FIRST TIME IN 1987. IT WAS PRETTY THRILLING BECAUSE I'D JUST STARTED GOING TO HARDCORE PUNK SHOWS AND I LIVED ON THE STREET FOR A TIME. I USED TO SLEEP BEHIND THE EL MOCAMBO."
JENNY SNOT

"IT WASN'T LIKE THE HELLS ANGELS, YOU'VE GOTTA HAVE YOUR COLOURS TYPE OF THING. EVERYBODY HAD THEIR OWN JACKET BUT THERE WAS NO INSIGNIA YOU HAD TO GO BUY AND YOU DIDN'T HAVE TO HAVE A BUNCH OF GOOFS GOING ACROSS YOUR JACKET. IF YOU WANTED IT, YOU DID IT; IF YOU DIDN'T, YOU DON'T."
SCUMBAG

"WE DIDN'T NEED MOTORCYCLES, WE DIDN'T NEED CARS. WE NEEDED SOMETHING FAST, LIGHT AND QUICK."
VIC NOTORIOUS

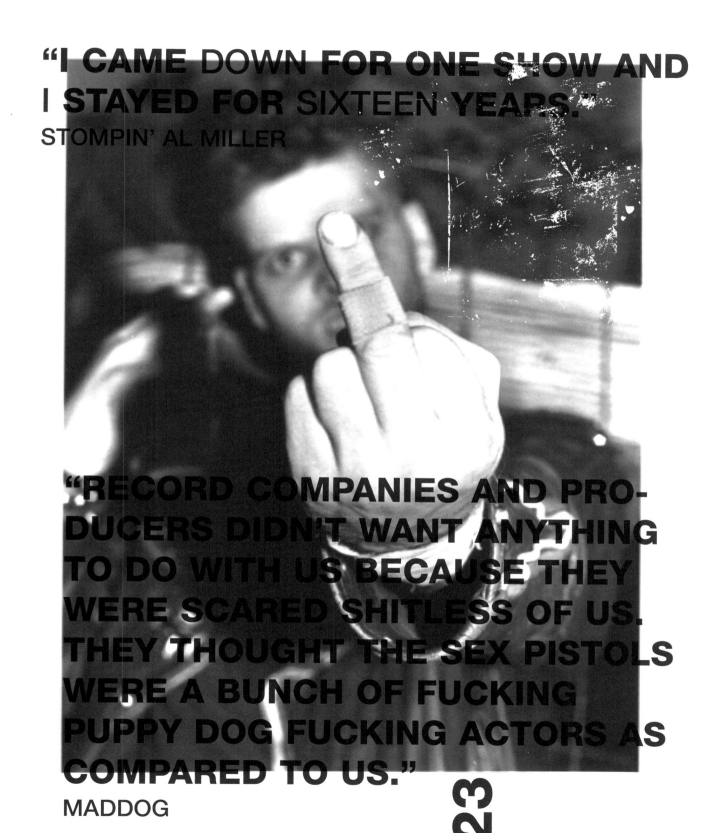

"I CAME DOWN FOR ONE SHOW AND I STAYED FOR SIXTEEN YEARS."
STOMPIN' AL MILLER

"RECORD COMPANIES AND PRODUCERS DIDN'T WANT ANYTHING TO DO WITH US BECAUSE THEY WERE SCARED SHITLESS OF US. THEY THOUGHT THE SEX PISTOLS WERE A BUNCH OF FUCKING PUPPY DOG FUCKING ACTORS AS COMPARED TO US."
MADDOG

TESTING TUBES
PUTTING US DOWN
ANDROPOV   TOGETHE
TRUE DOUGH

BUISS NESSCUM   STEVE
BITS & PIECES   TALK
                     (INTRO

LAUGHING   FAS
EXPLODING GLUE BAGS
MOON UNIT 2

DESTROY
KAL 007
CREATING CRIMINALS
SECOND HALF OF PIGS

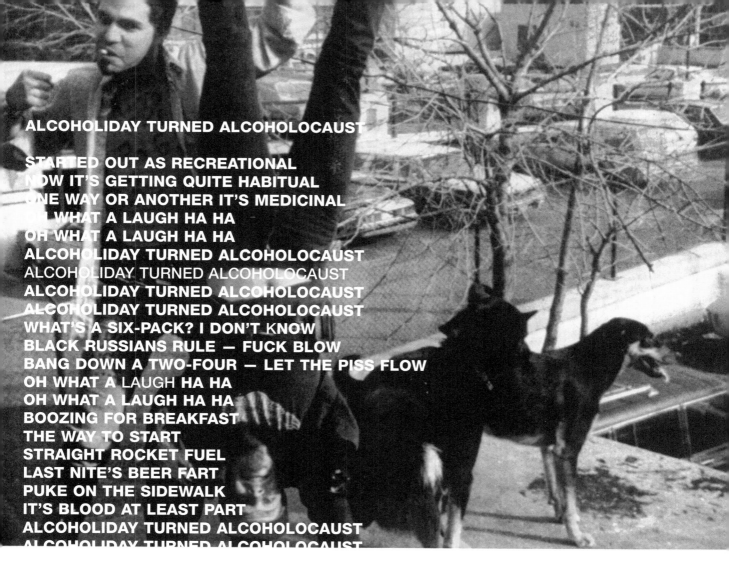

ALCOHOLIDAY TURNED ALCOHOLOCAUST

STARTED OUT AS RECREATIONAL
NOW IT'S GETTING QUITE HABITUAL
ONE WAY OR ANOTHER IT'S MEDICINAL
OH WHAT A LAUGH HA HA
OH WHAT A LAUGH HA HA
ALCOHOLIDAY TURNED ALCOHOLOCAUST
ALCOHOLIDAY TURNED ALCOHOLOCAUST
ALCOHOLIDAY TURNED ALCOHOLOCAUST
ALCOHOLIDAY TURNED ALCOHOLOCAUST
WHAT'S A SIX-PACK? I DON'T KNOW
BLACK RUSSIANS RULE — FUCK BLOW
BANG DOWN A TWO-FOUR — LET THE PISS FLOW
OH WHAT A LAUGH HA HA
OH WHAT A LAUGH HA HA
BOOZING FOR BREAKFAST
THE WAY TO START
STRAIGHT ROCKET FUEL
LAST NITE'S BEER FART
PUKE ON THE SIDEWALK
IT'S BLOOD AT LEAST PART
ALCOHOLIDAY TURNED ALCOHOLOCAUST
ALCOHOLIDAY TURNED ALCOHOLOCAUST
OH WHAT A LAUGH HA HA
OH WHAT A LIFE HA HA
OH WHAT A JOKE HA HA

Filthy
Sean

"It was an extremely ugly, messy, weird, night-marish story."

Rick McGinnis

"There were a lot of unusual stories in that environment. Sean's story was probably one of the heavier ones."
Susana

"Sean was never in the band."
MadDog

"He was in a band called None Of Your Fucking Business."
Thor

"Sean's totally messed up his life; what do you expect? He was hurt, he was messed up and he got in with the wrong people. He was somebody who really needed to belong. He brought a lot of it on himself too, but it's probably not the best thing in the world to kill your parents when you're fifteen, but what are you going to do?"
Greenie

"Sean, from what I know, when he was pretty young, killed his parents when he was fourteen. They were abusive, from what I know."
Thor

"He lived in St. Stephen, New Brunswick. His father had MS,
was in a wheelchair, small town, like nowhere land. The mother
was screwing the town preacher. Everybody in town knew what was
going on. He was, like, thirteen or fourteen. Went and got dad's
shotgun and he did a mercy killing . . . bitch."
Crazy Steve Goof

"There was alcoholism and there was violence. The family situation was really screwed up. His father kept telling him, 'When I get really sick—I want you to kill me.'"
Susana

"His father, who had a death wish, encouraged him. That was put upon a child, to help commit suicide essentially because his father couldn't do it anymore for himself. Then his mother and a third person were involved, as you know, which makes the whole scene so crazy."
Susana

"He was a young offender."
Crazy Steve Goof

"He was obviously pretty traumatized by those events, and he spent a long time in juvenile lock-up type stuff, and then they let him out."
Susana

"He got his education in there."
Thor

"The inheritance got split between Sean, his lawyer and his grandmother. He took that money and bought recording equipment."
Mopa Dean

"I'd been hanging out for about a year and Sean inherited money, quite a bit of money, if I recall, and all of a sudden Fort Goof was flush because he was sharing the money with the guys."
Rick McGinnis

"Sean started Back Alley Records and used the old British American Petroleum [B/A] as the logo. That was the label in and around BFG."
Mopa Dean

"Suddenly they were able to all afford rounds and poor Sean was usually shit-faced at this point. He helped pay for recording equipment that they had."
Rick McGinnis

"He put it into making a sort of an underground record company."
Thor

"You know, maybe blowing all your money on beer and Fort Goof wasn't a wise decision, but it seemed to me that it was the latest in a series of probably not wise decisions that Sean had made in life."
Rick McGinnis

"He could be a really loyal friend and a really funny guy to be around. He was, through his own description, a binge alcoholic. He either didn't drink at all or when he did drink, he would just drink to the gutter. He had good reason: like life had turned him some very difficult pieces."
Susana

"He was missing his right fucking finger. It was gone, completely got shot off with a shotgun."
Thor

"He was also open about that part of his history.
At least he was when I first met him. He came to the city and
started dealing with people, and I think, consciously or unconsciously,
he was like, 'Okay, let's get the worst part over with! Let's not build
a relationship and then have people freaked out.'"
Susana

"And all things considered, he was kind of together."
Thor

"Sean used to lean over when he was drunk and somebody was
annoying him: he would say, 'Quit bugging me cos I only need to kill
one more person to be a mass murderer.' He was doing it for the shock
effect. In actual fact, you never got the vibe off Sean that that was
something he would do, that's why the psychiatrist, the courts and
everybody else released him."
Susana

"He was just such a lost thing, so young, so much promise there, and
it's just kind of never materialized."
Greenie

"I don't think he was or is a danger. He was put into an insane situation."
Susana

"I don't really know what happened with Sean in the end.
I was sort of finding him such a tragic kid.
He made me kind of sad to be around him."
Rick McGinnis

"Good luck trying to find Sean."
Mopa Dean

Get A Bike – Asshole

We don't have to pay for gas
It's only funny when we crash
We don't need to buy insurance
A Kryptonite lock is the best defence
Traffic laws were made for cars
No charges coming back from bars
Depreciation does not exist
No car payments for us to meet or miss

We're out of here—we're moving fast
Without a bike you'll get there last
You can't expect anybody to wait
To wait for you would make us late

Gimme two wheels and no motor
And I'll show you what this road is for
Cut me off and I'll kick in your door
Scratch your paint and make you cry and feel real fucking sore

Filthy cars and their stinking fumes
Crowd the road and leave no room
No respect these clowns don't care
They're more worried about messing up their hair

Over the legal limit you have to take a cab
You should have paid off my beer tab
If you were as rude and stupid and foolish as them
You'd drive your car home and kill all of your fucking friends

So get a bike asshole and learn to really drive
But keep your eyes wide open if you wanna stay alive
So park your car and get off your fat ass
Or I'll give you the middle finger in traffic
As I —laugh — I laugh ha! ha! I laugh and sail past

Fort Goof [1985 – 91]
By Lynn Crosbie

They told me that he was bad, but I knew he was sad,
I'll never forget him – the leader of the pack
– The Shangri-las

I had met him before, opening a car with a coat hanger, other times.
He and his big dog, Dirt, all of them roaming the streets on skateboards,
Bicycles, in armour [chain belts, big black boots]. That he slept in a cage, in
A space fortressed by electrical wire, gangplank entrance off Baldwin Street.
Skittering across this in high heels, night after night, half in love.

Coming over after-hours, standing on the slag-roof by the hills of wheels
Spokes metal cans one derelict Mercedes, two stars visible he spills peach
Schnapps into my mouth from his, bliss.

Wet muzzles of dogs on my ankles, random killings. Trying to keep a low
Profile for almost seven years. Coaxing him to read his lyrics for us, my
Head on the dog's belly, a long flowered dress:

started out as recreational / now it's getting quite habitual –

to draw him like a hermit crab outside of himself. Kick this. Be a man for
once in your life and see me to the door. Kick that, higher.

With inappropriate presents of lavender bath salts and white roses,

chocolate hearts in foil; the night he has planned to have me [and five
scared friends] thrashed for violating the code. I'm heat score, he says
and I smile. His friends paw the floors, anxious.

Later he falls to his knees I'm sorry I'm sorry, drunk he would
save my life, several times, film me in handcuffs, Cisco coming up the stairs
looking for some action in Goofs Take 29; I am merely holding the cuffs
and am therefore not compromising myself, I say. It is 6 A.M. and time to
weave out through the alleys.

in my gown I am quite soignée, and I have a little lie down in an alley before
two kind policemen pick me up and drive me home. I imagine that there
were rats, lying like tiny babies in my arms,

like dolls: pills and drinking less and less food: alcoholiday turned
alcoholocaust, the song that he read when I lay in that gutter [looking
at the stars & c.]

Besieged by skinheads [we are 138 strong and will kill you], I see a little
crown when I pass by where it ended and began. With sledgehammers and
chainsaws, his eyes looking ahead, somewhere clear,

a clean table, plexiglass shower, plants in casement window. I am invited to
Dirt's wake this May. With more flowers, a round of toasts to the dog that
died in Mexico, lolling in the sun and startled by all the water, the purity.

Clean white bed he slips neatly into each night, hair still shaved in the one
thin line.

I crossed to meet him, like a pirate wild for the black flag,

that signals danger, night riders, the other marauder

who turns around and smiles at you, over shark fins, water as black as your
treacherous heart.

From the book *Queen Rat* [1998]

CHAPTER - FORT

[TITLE:] **FORT GOOF**
[SUBTITLE:] **IT WAS A BUNKER FULL OF PUNKS**

It's a miracle Crazy Steve Goof managed to convince someone to rent him a space he'd later stuff with Punks, dogs and booze can hounds. The first Fort was a one-bedroom apartment on the second floor of a rundown house at the end of a laneway in Kensington Market. The only way in was up the back fire escape.

They came up with the idea of cages at the Baldwin Street Fort. Like the market shops that used steel storefront fences to cover their doors when they closed, the Goofs surrounded their beds with cages, and then threw chains and padlocks around them. They divided up the space and gave themselves and their dogs a secure place to sleep. That way, no one jumped in their cages and tried to sell their mattresses. "My cage was four feet wide and in the hallway and stopped ten inches below the ceiling, and you could literally shimmy over it," says Kirk. "So I put barbed wire and razor wire across the top of it, so nobody would crawl through." Remember, home for these guys was a booze can where people drank all day and all night. Just because they wanted to sleep, didn't mean the party stopped.

Crazy Steve Goof's space in particular was described as having a Hugh Hefner kind of vibe to it. [Steve met at least fifteen SUNshine Girls]. His bed was round and he had red sheets with black skulls. He got the bed and the sheets from the street, like most other things in the Fort. Couches, chairs, tables…they were the leading edge of reduce, reuse and recycle. Graffiti was how they fluffed the place. Any money they made went back into the collective to pay for food, beer and renting amplifiers. It wasn't pretty. But that was the point.

The first Fort was also a recording studio, and a rehearsal space, and in some ways, a dog pound, with as many as nine guys and a dozen dogs living there at one point. In some areas, you couldn't stand up straight. Bambi was the first girl to live with the boys. There was one bathroom and no TV. There were no dishes in the sink. There was no sink.

"There were times that the front door didn't work, so you had to crawl through the roof of the toilet, and then there wasn't running water," says Greenie. "One summer we had to go down to Scadding Court - the local community centre - to bathe. The Fort had really horrible living conditions at times, but you know, everybody survived."

THE KITCHEN
AT THE BALDWIN FORT.

FILTHY SEAN'S "HOUSE"
AT THE BALDWIN FORT.

"INSTEAD OF THE DOGS LIVING IN CAGES, WE LIVED IN CAGES." — MICUS

Empty tallboys of Molson Export (the only beer ever served at the Fort) were tossed off the roof down onto a pile fifteen feet below, into a backyard full of thousands of bicycle parts. Before the cans were loaded into shopping carts and brought back for five cents each, the drunks dove off the roof into the metal mattress for fun.

The door to the first Fort on Baldwin was like an old bank safe. Keep in mind, attacks on Punk houses happened, especially from Nazi Skinheads.

Most people would come into the Fort from the back, but they were still worried about someone breaking into the Fort through the window that faced the street. So they welded a huge set of bars and caging over the window frame, held onto the wall by four, ten-inch long bolts that went right through the cinderblock walls from the outside of the building to the inside. There was a strip of carpet in front of the window; at night they would open the window and pour water on the carpet. Then, they ran an electrical current from an outlet to those ten-inch bolts. So anyone who tried to mess with the windows got a nice jolt. Not enough to do any major internal damage, just enough to mess them up for a bit.

What's a Fort without a lookout? The Goofs replaced a skylight at the Baldwin Fort with a giant, forty-gallon stainless steel mixing bowl – the kind bakers use to mix huge batches of dough. They cut a six-by-two-inch slit in the bowl, poured concrete on the roof to hold it in place and so no one could dig underneath it. You had to climb a ladder in the bathroom to look through it. They attached one piece of chain to the underside of the bowl, and another to the floor and pulled them tight when they wanted to seal everything shut. The bowl rotated 360 degrees so they could see who was coming from every angle.

And what's a Fort without a doctor? When MadDog wasn't building cages or finding ways to electrocute intruders, he would tend to the Punk flock. Before he was MadDog, Kirk was known as the Mad Doc. Not because he had any medical training, but because he'd been in the care of medical professionals so many times, he'd picked up their tricks and applied his learned skills to people, and even dogs, in the scene.

"I just knew about medical stuff from being smashed up and sewn up so many times in my life," says MadDog. "I'd had it done to me so many times, I became an expert at it.

He happened to have a medical bag full of gauze, tape, suture thread and ordinary sewing needles. He would "repair" Punks, especially at Punkfest. Even stitched up the torn hind leg of a pit bull after it got in a fight with another dog.

40

Ontario

SHERIFF'S NOTICE

BY VIRTUE of a certain Writ of Possession to me directed, I have executed

the said Writ as commanded and restored possession of the Lands and

Premises known as: _173 BALDWIN STREET, TORONTO_

To: _THE LANDLORD_

For removal of goods contact Tel # _555-3553_

RICHARD

AND FURTHER TAKE NOTICE that anyone who enters without the

express consent of the above commits a trespass and is liable to prosecution

under the provisions of the Criminal Code of Canada.

Dated this _12th_ day of _APRIL_   19_88_

Sheriff
Judicial District of York

THE BOYS WITH ACID BUNNY, OXFORD FORT
Photo by Miki Toma

"IT WAS A BEAT OR BE BEATEN, EAT OR BE EATEN KIND OF THING. SO YOU FIGHT AND DRINK AND FUCK AND SLEEP ON THE FLOOR."

— MADDOG

MadDog/Doc eventually became – unofficially – the Mad Dentist. "A couple of people had bad teeth and they were complaining about them for days, and I'd said 'Fuck, I'll pull the fucking thing out for ya,'" says MadDog. "I'd sterilize my pair of needle-nosed, curled pliers so I can get in on the tooth, and yank her out. I'd make them slam back a few beers, and pop a couple of pills and yank the sucker out."

MadDog had his teeth yanked out in pretty much the same way – in his case by an actual dentist – and figured he knew what he was doing.

"It's the same thing a doctor did to me . . . . The doctor would go in, twist it to get it loose and pull it out. I had that done four times, so after that, I went, 'Fuck it, I'll just twist your tooth to get it a little bit loose and pop her out,'" says MadDog. "There's no guarantee it's coming out in one piece, but both times they came out in one piece...beautiful pulls, just like a doctor would do."

THE 24-HOUR CARNIVAL OF CHAOS AND CARNAGE CONTINUES . . .

44

Before moving to the second Fort, the Goofs organized a teardown party. Everything was destroyed or painted over. They painted everything black because they felt the graffiti was too personal to leave behind.

The second, Oxford Street Fort in the Market was bigger and better. They called the 3,200 square feet basement of a four-storey warehouse, Goofworld. Again, Steve managed to convince someone to rent him the space. It was an old booze can that burnt to crap. It was dark, dirty and needed a shower and toilet. Once again, they scavenged the streets for couches, tables and chairs. Unlike the first Fort, this one had doors, so they used casket handles for doorknobs. MadDog built everything, including the new cages. Thor picked up his brushes and comic-booked the walls. There were three doors of security before you could get inside. The first had a dead bolt and some slidebolts; the other two sets of swinging doors had four slidebolts and two drop-bars. The windows were replaced with plywood. Only one window was able to open...for an emergency exit...and it was kept secret.

When they moved in, a list of rules was made and duct-taped to the back of the front door. They wanted to make sure everybody had it straight from the start.

Don't smash bottles
Don't piss in neighbours' doorways
Don't take taxis to the front of the building
Don't bring people you don't know
Don't hang around outside

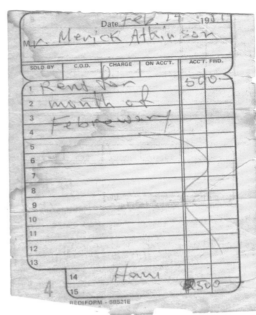

Don't cause a heat score

RAT WARS

The elevator was full of rats, and the Goofs fixed it so it couldn't reach the Fort. As soon as they moved in, the rat war began. Rodent versus radical, both fighting for survival and scavenging for turf in a place neither should have been living.

To keep the rat pack at bay, the Goofs plugged their holes with steel wool and cement, and finally barbed wire. But that didn't stop them. They shot them with pellet guns and used the dogs to chase them out, but in the end it was Simon's ferret that killed them all. Problem solved.

"When we first moved into the second Fort, there was no plumbing," recalls Thor. "We ended up building a bathroom, using old school lockers, and made a shower stall. We took a big blue water jug with the valve on it, filled it up with freezing cold water and poured it on ourselves. Then you'd soap up, pour a little more on and rinse off. That was our shower."

EVEN THE COPS NEEDED AN INVITE TO GET INTO THE FORT

The cops knew about the Fort and stayed away, but sometimes they came by to check on things. The first Fort had three steel fire doors sandwiched together with a layer of stainless steel on top and a spider bolt locking system on the inside. One night when they were blowing up "bombs" made of cordite and cardboard tubes from old shotguns shells in the backyard, the cops showed up. The Goofs listened in on scanner radios. They heard the cop talking to his sergeant saying he couldn't find a way to get in through the door, that the battering ram he had wouldn't work and asking his boss what he should do. The sergeant said, "Forget about it, go home." The cop did. And the Goofs laughed their asses off about it.

Like the band, the Oxford Street Fort eventually blew up. "The core group moved away and it turned into a kind of hotel," says Crazy Steve Goof. "It became what it wasn't supposed to be…a business."

The Jamaicans started running a booze can upstairs that wasn't to Steve's liking. They broke his rules…no idling taxis, no security on walkie-talkies, no noise. The neighbours were to be respected, and these new guys didn't. They drew heat and attention. The end of the Fort involved a two-by-four and a broken promise. Steve showed up one night after being away on tour to find a competing booze can taking place above the Fort. He crashed in wielding a two-by-four with a hammer in his pocket. He emptied out the booze can and chased forty guys down the street. That night, a guy's teeth were broken, along with a nose and a couple of fingers. Steve left town for a while, without a scratch.

TOTAL TEARDOWN

"We wanted to fuckin' kill it."

— CRAZY STEVE GOOF

Stills taken from 16mm film Total Breakdown by Steev Morgan, March 1988

FORT BALDWIN was built out of crazy creativity and destroyed with that very same force. For five years it was their clubhouse until one day the landlord said, "Enough" and kicked them out. Their answer: "Fuck you." They decided to hold a demolition party with Crazy Steve Goof, MadDog and Filthy Sean doing most of the honours. It was partly fun and partly necessary. Over the years, thousands of people, dogs, bikes and beers had passed through the place. The walls were message boards smothered thick with anti-police slogans and phone numbers. The insides of cabinets were phone books and the place they recorded people's beer tabs. They had to destroy any and all evidence of what had gone on there. So they tore it all down and painted every inch of it flat black, so no clues were left for the police or anyone else. They also didn't want anyone else to live in the Punk palace they created. After moving into the new Fort on Oxford and discovering they needed wood to build walls, the Goofs — wearing balaclavas and women's stockings over their heads — broke back into to the old Fort on Baldwin, and scooped up all the two-by-fours.

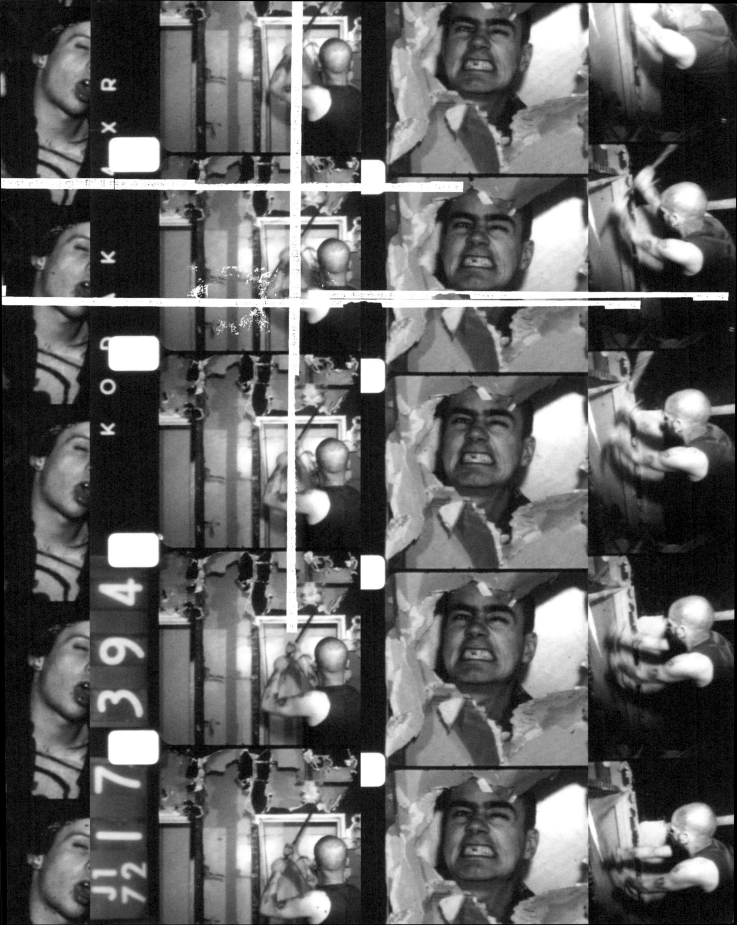

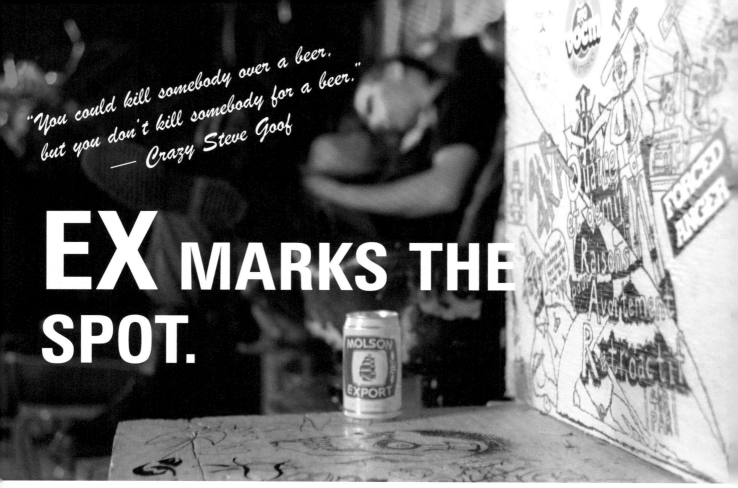

"You could kill somebody over a beer, but you don't kill somebody for a beer."
— Crazy Steve Goof

EX MARKS THE SPOT.

BFG BEER FACTS AND STATS

· Steve says they probably sold around half a million cans of beer.
· They bought at least ten cases of beer every day.
· Molson Export was the Punk beer of choice.
· Cans only, never bottles; the dogs might cut their feet on the glass.
· Sold them for $2 each or three for $5.
· The rule was sell them for double what they cost at the beer store.
· They kept the beer in an old 1950s Pepsi cooler.
· Aside from the cages, the only thing in the Forts with a lock was the beer fridge.
· The beer fridge was also the cash register; the cold hard cash was kept in the freezer.
· All the Goofs had beer pockets sewed into their jackets.
· Steve kept a record of how many beers Scumbag owed him for, written up, down and along walls of the Fort. Total: 1,059.
· Beer was used as currency.
· Thor did tattoos in exchange for beer.
· Steve could and often did, drink a case of beer (or more) in a day.
· They would bag the empties and throw them off the roof and dive into them.
· At one point the pile was made up of 4,137 cans.

PART OF THE MARKET

"THEY FIT RIGHT INTO THE COMMUNITY. KENSINGTON IS A CRAZY PLACE. I'VE LIVED HERE ALL MY LIFE. THE FIRST COUPLE OF WEEKS THEY WERE HERE, THEY USED TO LIVE ACROSS THE STREET, PEOPLE GAVE THEM THE ODD 'THOSE GUYS LOOK PRETTY STRANGE...' BUT I MEAN, THEY FIT RIGHT IN. THEY'RE PART OF THE MARKET."

— BUTCHER, KENSINGTON MARKET

FROM *THE NEWMUSIC* [CITYTV] APRIL 1989 EPISODE ON THE BUNCHOFUCKINGOOFS,
PRODUCED BY JENNIFER MORTON.

Crazy Steve Goof and Filthy Sean at the butchers.

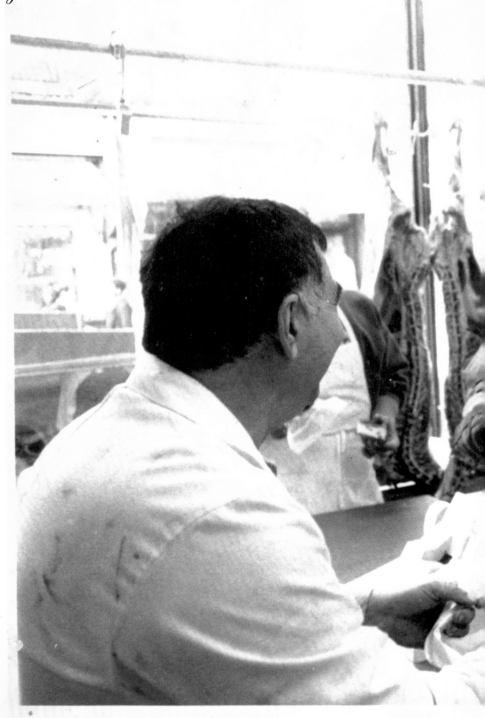

We are Family

I Got All My Punkers And Me . . .

MEMBERSHIP HAS ITS PRIVILEGES

"Most people were outcasts, people who just didn't fit in, people who lived on the street, people who said, 'Screw you if you aren't going to accept me.'"
— THOR —

"I think for some people it's feeling rejected and saying, well all right, you can't reject me 'cause I reject you. Screw you."
— MOPA DEAN —

"I'm First Nations and there was so much I could relate to. 'You're angry? Me too. You're being oppressed? So am I.'"
— JENNY SNOT —

"Cultish? How do you define a cult? You could leave if you wanted to; it wasn't like you were brainwashed. It was more like Andy Warhol's warehouse space down in New York.
— COLLEEN SUBASIC —

"The Goofs had this guy Cisco, who back then was probably in his late fifties. He was an old Rochdale hippie; he used to be a cop in Uruguay. And he was in the band. He used to light the stage on fire, or pull out machetes. Cisco was one of the nicest people around. He was accepted into the same crowd that I was."
— CITIZEN GREG —

"I got kicked out of my house when I was thirteen years old. Eventually I got welfare to rent me a room and it ended up being at Larry's Hideaway; room 228. I was hanging out there and listening to all this Punk rock music, and the bouncers are calling me a little fucking kid and telling me stay in my fucking room. They got to know me and would sneak me in the back door. Eventually I ran into Steve Goof and MadDog and they were like, 'You wanna come to our place?' I said yeah, and never left."
— SCUMBAG —

FAMILY TIES

"A lot of young kids living on the streets were taken care of. The Goofs helped kids come together and meet each other so they could afford to have a place to stay. Steve was kind of a counsellor."
— COLLEEN SUBASIC —

"At least there was a purpose, which is people not being fucked up, people actually getting off of bad drugs, people actually thinking that they're worth something, people actually working to get out of the pit that they're in without sucking corporate cock, without sucking the government's cock."
— BONES —

"I grew up in a cult called Therafields. I loved the insanity of the Goofs.
It was the only thing that I was used to and it was comforting to me. I always think
of what the alternatives might have been."
— SCRAG —

"I've certainly wondered over the years what attracted me into that situation.
In my own life I came from a family that could be described as — dysfunctional. I think
for a lot of kids that were involved in the whole Punk scene, there's anger that's
being played out in the music, how they dress and how they behave.
— SUSANA —

"I learned how to cook from the guys. When I moved in, they had an
electric frying pan and a hot plate."
— TARATARATARA —

"One time, I'm getting ready to leave the Fort, and I see this guy passed out.
Then another guy comes up and puts a blanket over him, and makes sure his head's
turned so if he pukes, he's not going to choke. It gave me a sense of their bond.
The bond of a bunch of fucking goofs."
— CARSON T. FOSTER —

"They're productive members of society. Just because you don't wear a suit
doesn't mean to say you're not producing. They work, they earn their own living.
They're not living off people."
— STEWART SCRIVER —

"There were fights and stuff like that at the Fort, but if there were problems,
they worked it out and, just like with all gangs, justice was meted out and nothing bad
happens if you're part of the clan. Probably clan's a better word than cult."
— COLLEEN SUBASIC —

KENSINGTON MARKET: THEIR HOME AND SACRED LAND

"There were so many visible minority groups in the area,
we immediately became another one."
— CRAZY STEVE GOOF —

"I refer to the Market as the black hole of Toronto. The Market pulls you in
somehow because it's a safe place. You have to be really bizarre to stand out in the
Market. It's a place where everybody belongs. A lot of the Goofs and the people that
hung around them were united in the fact that they didn't really care for the way
society was going and so they created their own world."
— STEWART SCRIVER —

"I don't think [the Goof scene] could have existed anywhere else in the city.
It had to be in the Market. The Market's the vortex."
— MIKE SMALLSKI —

Party at Dawn Mourning's, 1986

Thor, Dirt, Crazy Steve Goof

"Steve is Big Brother. If anybody has a problem they go to him. If he can help you, he'll help you. It's the same with the other guys. They watch over the stores at night. If they see anything they stop it. I've seen trouble break out in this neighbourhood and it's been Steve and the other guys that have come to the rescue. We had a big problem with the crackheads and the place that used to sell cocaine down the street. People called the cops. Nothing happened. Steve and some of the Goofs, started following [the crackheads] saying 'Hey, this is a drug dealer,' pointing at them and embarrassing them."

— OSSIE —

"We picked through the garbage at night. There was lots of good food; we ate well. We made great fruit salads. And all the veggies that were slightly bruised, we'd cut out the bad parts and, like, make huge stir-fries and have a feast."

— MIKE SMALLSKI —

"We'd get a giant wok and rice and vegetables and feed thirty Punks off the street."

— VIC NOTORIOUS —

"They were like one short step away from being street people, but they weren't. Some of the original Goofs, I see them every day, I'm amazed they're still around."

— STEWART SCRIVER —

"We raised a child in the Market and I always felt it was one of the safer places in the city with those guys around. I pity the guy who tries to rob or vandalize a shop when the Goofs are around."

— JOHN BORRA —

BANISHMENT

"We didn't just let anybody in. And if anybody fucks up, they're banished. You're not just banished from our place, you're banished from our shows, you're banished from the scene. Leave town, don't be seen around, don't show up at a show, don't show up at a party, don't show up nowhere or you're going to get pounded."

— MADDOG —

"You have to be able to pull your weight and keep your shit together and not fuck up everybody else. You have to be able to go out and deal with the public and not make everybody else in the band look bad. We can't have people with BFG on the back of their jackets running around in bars causing trouble because that reflects badly on all the rest of us. So we don't allow people like that to hang around us. Keep it together or take a walk."

— CRAZY STEVE GOOF —

"We more or less had our own court, and if you fucked up, you knew to a certain degree what the repercussions were going to be. You do something seriously fucked up or bad and you're going to get pounded or you're going to be banished."

— MADDOG —

(Top) Crazy Steve Goof and Co. at The Apocalypse Club, (Bottom left) Thor and Booze, (Bottom right) Scumbag

"We were playing a show at the Generator, opening up for the DayGlo Abortions.
I had just got off stage and was talking to some people, and the next thing you know
I was on the ground. Steve suckerpunched me. That was the last time he ever hit me.
After that I had to leave Toronto."
— DROOL —

RE-BRANDING THEMSELVES

"My close friends call me Kator. And at some point in time, the band came up with
terrorist names for each other for a laugh. That's when I became al-Qaetor."
— KATY —

"At first I was the Mad Doctor. I used to always carry, like, a black medical bag with all
my stuff in it. Still, I was a kind of a doctor. If someone got fucked up I'd fix them up, I
had bags and bags of band-aids. Also, I became the doctor because I trashed myself so
much through my life and I knew trauma and what to do about most trauma. Then everybody called me Mad Doc. When I got in the band, people started calling me MadDog."
— MADDOG —

"A lot of people came and went. You never knew most people's real names. Like Dopey,
we gave him that name. He was always trying to change it but we ignored him."
— GREENIE —

"I wanted to be Bob, so I said 'I'm Be Bob, like it or leave it. I'm the happy big guy and I'll
punch you out if you don't like it.' And that's how it came, to be or not to be, I will be Bob."
— B. BOB —

One poor guy got stuck with Dopey. Citizen Greg got his name cos he was an
upstanding member of the community. King Kong was an obvious choice for a
huge (in every way) dude who liked to dress up in clown costumes. He also went
by Big Jamie and occasionally Fisty the Clown. TaraTaraTara got her nickname
from Steve. Godzilla (God for short) was also huge. Greenie always wore green
or dyed her mohawk green. *NOW* magazine wrote an article on the Goofs and
by mistake under the photo wrote Greg Goose, instead of Goof. That was it.
Greg became Goose after that. Jenny Snot (now Jenny Blackbird) got her name
from Steve when he helped cast her in the *War of the Worlds* TV series. He didn't
know her last name and told the casting director it was Snot. Tanya Cheex
(Jenny Snot's friend) who was tall, blonde and wore lots of pink, also went by
Feelin' Shitty Barbie. Her inspiration was Feelin' Groovy Barbie. Steve was
sometimes called Johnny by his inner circle, seeing as how his long-long last
name is Johnson. Filthy Sean was also called Nine-Finger(s) because he blew
one of them off with a shotgun. (Drool thought Filthy Sean was the coolest guy
on the planet.) Barronwasteland's real name was Aaron; the wasteland part came
from *Road Warrior*. Gymbo Jak and Mike Jak named themselves after the "Jak"
skateboard collective.

(Top right) Anna Banana and MadDog

66

Bambi on

Bambi

Bambi ran from the suburbs to the city. A brutal fight broke out between the Skins and The Goofs in the house where she was crashing. She couldn't stay there any longer, and friends told her about Fort Goof. With nothing to lose, she climbed up the fire escape and asked if she could stay. Bambi was the first girl to live at the Fort and the first guitar player for the BFGs. She was funny, creative, wild and a little messed up. MadDog summed her up like this, "She got some shit together, she got hammered with us, she got high with us, she hung out with us and everything. She was a cool person." Bambi has since split Toronto.

From 1983-1984, director Edward Mowbray shot *Not Dead Yet*, a documentary film about the year in the life of the hardcore Toronto Punk scene that featured Bambi and Crazy Steve Goof.

69

"It's sad that
you have to be a rebel
to be free."

ON LEAVING THE BAND

It was devastating. It changed my life. It blew me outta the water. It was a wake-up call and that's probably what their goal was. It's too bad that I had to be dealt with that harshly. I don't think I deserved that. I was not a bad person. I just showed up at the door one day. There was a big guy standing in the door and he smiled at me and we shook hands. I was like, who are you? I can't remember the conversation, but I went into the house and asked somebody about the rehearsal and they said that they had a new guitar player and that I wasn't playing. I just snapped.

I guess carving up my arms or carving upside down crosses in my chest in front of the guys at the Fort. Wearing pajamas on the street or not bathing for a week. I guess those could have been part of it. Or walking around with needles hangin' out of my arms.

They don't hate me. They know in their hearts that I am good, you know.

I was just a kid. I was a runaway. I was a liar. I stole. I was investigating every possible illegal outlet I could. Just living to the fullest. The bad and the good. You know sex, drugs and rock and roll — these were the good things.

I don't know what my mission was. Maybe to be notorious, maybe to be famous, maybe to be infamous. If I'd stayed at ballet I'd probably be a famous dancer. If I'd stayed with the conservatory piano maybe I'd be famous right now. But all the energy I had I put into being a clown or a warrior or a goof.

You know, I loved those guys and I had to leave the city cos there was a big war and I was on the wrong side. People started to attack me on the street and threaten me. I called Steve and asked him to call off the dogs. He said, 'What makes you so sure they are mine?' He had the power

in my opinion to stop that. I had to go out on my own. I left everyone. I left the city. I had my life threatened.

There was always a lineup outside of Steve's door. The odd time he'd ask me to help him reduce that problem. He'd fool people into thinking we were going out. Steve was asked about what love had to do with Punk. Steve said, "You know Punk is drinking. Punk is fighting. Punk is fucking. Punk has nothing to do with love."

I remember Kirk [MadDog] holdin' a gun, like a rifle in his loft hallway. I walked down the hallway one day and he had a gun pointing at my forehead. I got scared. Steve comes through and walks right up to the gun barrel and puts it right on his face and then moved it, glaring at Kirk. "You're scaring my dog," he goes. I hate guns. I had a sawed-off one in my room but it didn't work.

Tinkleuk used to shoot cockroaches off the walls. He'd come in all smashed and fall on me and his dog would jump on my face. We shared the same bed for a while. We weren't going out or nothing. He'd crash on me and pull out his rifle and start blowing the clock away when it rang and the cock-roaches off the walls. These guys were way out there and it's cool. It made me feel safe, you know. I would have stopped a bullet for any of them.

I could put a song together. When the shit broke out between the Skinheads and them at the Fort that gave us all the writing material we needed for lyrics.

It was like a big brotherhood. It was fun to be around. I just loved them. Never a dull moment. After walking around the street all night or partying, I'd knock a code and go in and there'd be bodies lying all over the floor.

I first discovered Punk rock when I was fifteen, or fourteen maybe. I ran away from home when I was sixteen. I remember hearing the UK Subs and loving them. I started shaving my head 'cause the people I knew were into the Skinhead thing. I found out I wasn't interested in it. It was bullshit man, really twisted and sick. Beating people up for their boots and racial issues; what's

with this Hitler shit? I didn't understand, but they were my high school friends. I tried to find a common way for us to hang out together and it was Punk rock.

I was a liar and a stealer and a fighter not a drunk. That's why I put in a mother of a fucker of Punk.

CRAZY STEVE GOOF ON BAMBI

She was fuckin' hysterical. She was a fuckin' super, funny, crazy, fuckin' freak! I always liked Bambi. I remember when she used to wear pajamas all the time. It's a tradition I believe that was started earlier by these two girls on Berkeley Street in 1981. They shaved their heads and dressed like mental patients.

She had a bunch of tutus. And, the rest of her clothes…she'd safety-pin together, stencil and spray-paint them in different colours. Once, I scored a million bags of crazy coloured dye, and she take them, dye her clothing and her hair the same colour, and make that her outfit for the day. So it was fuckin' heavy. She used to do it all the time and it looked really fuckin' cool.

In the end she got really fucked up. She was hanging around with fuckin' Mike Nightmare from The Ugly who was a fuckin' serious freak. They were stealing doctors' bags filled with stupid, shitty pharmaceuticals, anything you could shoot up. In the end, she just sort of lost her mind and faded off.

Bambi interview excerpts taken from:
Not Dead Yet and *Punk X*
by Edward Mowbray
Courtesy Not Dead Yet & Victory Video Arts
© 1984

Sorry I ... s suck
guitarist and I a
a big problem an
and a bad phren
given. I was nut
A Big F. G.

a bad female
sorry for being
a bad person
Hope to be for-
n but a goof.

Sincerely,

Bambi

"IT WAS AN EXPERIENCE. I WOULDN'T VIEW IT AS POSITIVE OR NEGATIVE. I KIND OF LOOK AT IT AS A SOCIAL EXPERIMENT WHEN I STARTED IT. SO, THE EXPERIMENT KIND OF GOT OUT OF HAND AS FAR AS THAT GOES. BUT I WOULDN'T PUT IT AS POSITIVE OR NEGATIVE. BASICALLY, I WANTED TO SEE WHAT CRAZY PEOPLE DO. AND I REALIZED I'M MUCH CRAZIER THAN MOST."

MIKE STEAD

The Unwanted Sounds of

QUARANTINE

with

UNCHOFUCKINGOOFS

.P.B

rning Ring   UPPER
                       LIP
eceiver   SAT. DEC. 3rd.

First TORONTO APEARANCE

THE HINCKLY'S

JAILBAIT ADMITTED

...75..... .

PRE-PROGRAMMED

Stupid couch potatoes
You sit around
Watch the tube
Don't make a sound
Which show you watch
Does not matter
The ass you sit on
Gets even fatter

The crap you watch, your brain digests
You'll even watch the colour tests

The shit you watch
Lets them control
They've got your brain
Within their hold
You'll buy their products
And believe their shit
They'll make you look
Like a fucking tit

You'll vote for jerks, not even know why
The soaps you watch will make you cry

You don't have the parts
To live your life
You treat that set
Just like your wife
There are lots of ways
To spend your time
Watching that shit
Won't be mine

The crap you watch you don't even like
Turn off that set go ride your fucking bike

THE STORY OF
A MACHETE, A
AND A DEATH

7

MUCUS, LOST TESTICLE, WISH

GOOF *FOR LIFE*

"I wouldn't say getting my face caved in was a great way to meet people. It took twenty-three surgeries to get my face back. But it was a good thing, it was worth it. I met the best friends I've ever had."
Mucus

~~Mucus first met the Goofs when he was drinking—underage—at a b~~
~~he went to see the band again. It was a Friday night, and they were o~~
~~Augusta Street in Kensington Market. The Goofs launched into their la~~
~~and Thor was smashing them. Mucus was up front enjoying the chao~~
~~went flying into the crowd. It stopped when it hit Mucus's face.~~
     ~~If you're wondering how Mucus got his streetname…~~
~~He and a bunch of friends were playing pool at the old X Rays bar on~~
~~was cheating started calling him a faggot and a dirty Punk rocker (tha~~
~~When the guy kept yelling Mucus sneez l in his m   h   l kicked h~~

Mucus first met the Goofs when he was drinking — underage — at a bar in London, Ontario. Shortly after he moved to Toronto, he went to see the band again. It was a Friday night, and they were opening for the DayGlo Abortions at the Siboney Club on Augusta Street in Kensington Market. The Goofs launched into their last song, "Pre-Programmed." The stage was full of TVs and Thor was smashing them. Mucus was up front enjoying the chaos when the metal pipe slipped out of Thor's hand and went flying into the crowd. It stopped when it hit Mucus's face.

If you're wondering how **Mucus** got his streetname . . . He and a bunch of friends were playing pool at the old X-Rays bar on Queen Street West in Toronto. A guy who thought he was cheating started calling him a faggot and a dirty Punk rocker (thanks to his green hair), then punched Mucus in the nose. When the guy kept yelling Mucus sneezed in his mouth, and kicked him in the face as he started throwing up. A guy in a suit watching everything go down said, "Hey Mr. Mucus, do you want a beer?"

Mucus said sure. The name stuck.

"I show up after work around midnight hoping to catch the DayGlos 'cause I just missed the Goofs," recalls Citizen Greg. "I order a drink and go to the can, and there's blood everywhere. All over the can, and all down the hall. There's so much it's coagulating. I thought someone got murdered."

Greenie, a friend of the Goofs, grabbed Mucus and raced him to the emergency room at the Toronto Western Hospital. They didn't even know each other. Despite his injuries, he was so drunk no one there was in a hurry to help him. Greenie wouldn't let him look in the mirror. He'd lost half his face.

"Greenie saved my ass," says Mucus." "She gave me these homeopath things that coagulated my blood so instead of bleeding to death I stopped bleeding."

After the DayGlo Abortions finished their set, everyone went back to the Fort where the booze can was in full swing. Citizen Greg was bartending there that night. Thor told him this guy would be showing up and he was supposed to get all the free beer he wanted.

When he left the hospital, Greenie brought him back to the Fort. As soon as they saw Mucus they welcomed him in straight away.

"They're all screaming, 'You're the guy who got his face smashed, come on in!" says Mucus. "I got free beer all night, Greg was the bartender and that's how I met him." They used to live together in a tiny, smoke-filled apartment on Kensington Avenue with two dogs and a cat.

Mucus was awarded the status of being a Goof for life. He can drink for free and will never pay a cover at any BFG or DayGlo show.

HANGING AT THE FORT

"One night, this guy Steve (not Crazy Steve Goof) shows up at the Baldwin Fort, and he was telling me and Scumbag that he was going to kill himself. I watched a lot of people crash and burn. It was all horseshit. If you couldn't handle it, don't do it, right? We eventually got so tired of his dribble that we grabbed him, put a rope around his neck and hung him. We hung him 'til he turned blue and then we let him down. You should have seen the look in his eyes when he wasn't sure anymore what was going to happen. He didn't feel like dying anymore."

— Mucus

MUCUS

THOR & THE MACHETE

"We didn't call the cops. We didn't call anyone to the Fort. But if somebody was so injured that they had to be hospitalized, we'd throw them in a shopping cart and away they went to the hospital."

"One night I came home hammered, smashed, pissed drunk, and Dirt was there. You didn't mess with Dirt. Nobody messed with Dirt. He was a big, tough dog and he'd bite you. I grabbed Dirt and started wrestling with him, and people flipped out because nobody did that. Somebody runs to the Greeks, finds Steve and tells him I'm beating up his dog. Steve's drunk, loses it, and runs back to the Fort. By the time he gets there, I'm passed out on the couch. So he piles up all this furniture on top of me, grabs his hatchet and at the last minute, he flipped it around instead of hitting me with the blade. Split my head wide open.

"So they get a shopping cart and throw me in. They were wheeling me to the hospital when apparently I woke up, covered in blood, flipped out and I started climbing some building and freaking out like fucking King Kong. I ran through the building and out a window and the firemen and cops were called.

"I woke up in jail with staples in my head. The next time I saw Steve, he said he was sorry, I said, 'I understand, dude.' That's the way it was. Move on." — Thor

OUCH, **THAT** MUSTA HURT...

"Drool had done something really bad, and when Thor ran into him at a party, he walked up to him and they had words. Drool said the wrong thing and Thor hoofed him in the nuts. Literally sent him right out the window, and down two storeys. Drew ended up loosing a testicle during the trip." — MadDog

"No, no, no, I didn't fly out a second-storey window. That was at a different party, when Thor was trying to stop me from jumping off the balcony 'cause I'd jumped off it once or twice already. We were just having fun and we were completely out of our minds...different story. We were at a party and he sucker-punched this guy. I was so drunk and I got so angry that a guy the size of Thor should suckerpunch anybody. I ended up trying to fight him, which wasn't very smart, and that's where the kick to the nuts came from." — Drool

"It was justice that I think went a little bit too far, you know what I mean? I don't even think Thor meant to send him out the window but he kicked him so hard he sent him right out the fucking window. It was like, holy fuck." — MadDog

"We walked Drool back home that night but didn't realize he was in so much pain. The next day we had to take him to the hospital. What a sight. I loved it...Oh my God. The guys couldn't even look at it." — Greenie

ABOVE: THOR   BELOW: DROOL

Photo by Chris Buck

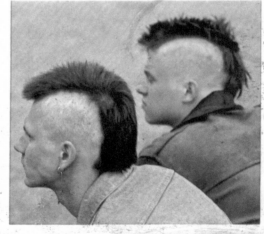

CEIPT FOR CAB

nt .... Date ....
47 Kensington Av.
o. 4 .... Driver 4
DO HOUSE CALLS 4
CO-OP CAB

NEW

WEEKEND PASS
SATURDAY PASS
SUNDAY PASS
1984

RTS COUNCIL   Volume

WEEKEND PASS

Basement
tapes
by B.F.G.

June

3 Monday

4 Tuesday   Meet S

5 Wednesday

Thursday   Order cab

Pick up tickets for B.F.G Band

F.G Concert

The heroes of youth range from
amuse themselves at the expense of a
city policeman (**facing page**). A counter
cult is the punkkarit—punks— (**above**),
whose tastes run to bizarre haircuts
and rock music played on a chain saw.

POSTER ART BY CISCO

Spend 1985 touring some of the most breathtaking wilderness

YOU HAD A CHOICE OF GETTING YOUR HAIR CUT OFF OR YOUR TEETH KICKED IN

THERE ARE NOT A LOT OF P U N K ROCK LOVE SONGS.

The BFGs never wrote one. They communicated through violence. It was how they expressed themselves. The first stories out of a lot of these Punkers' mouths usually involve blood and emergency rooms. Although a lot of the stories in this book are completely horrifying and brutal, they're remembered with pride. Life was hardcore, in your face, suck it up and shut up. It was all anarchic adventure. It was about standing up for your rights, not backing down and being ready for anything.

"Punk rock is a dangerous pastime," says Cretin. "I've broken the majority of the bones in my body: my back, my skull, most of my arms, my legs, my ribs, my hip . . ."

The Goofs wore Mad Max-style body armour. But it wasn't just about looking tough, it was about wearing their weapons: police calfguards worn high on the thigh to prevent charley horses, metal-studded bracelets, hose clamps worn as rings, knee pads, army boots and leather jackets with hidden pockets. Kryptonite bike locks came in handy…especially for blocking blows from a baseball bat.

"Our belts were chains, with seatbelt buckles," says Crazy Steve Goof. "Mine was made from three lengths of chain, and a quick release put on for the dog. When you unhooked the dog it became a thirty-inch length of chain. If you undid the other clip you'd have a ninety-inch piece of chain. All buckled up it weighed about twenty pounds. The padlock sat on the right side of your hip so when the button was pushed the chain fell in to your hand and the lock from the other side would hit the person in the head. It was an amazing, legal weapon."

NO LAWYERS, NO APPEALS, NO GRUDGES

One story has it that a kangaroo court was set up to decide the fate of a hippie (lovingly referred to as a "long hair") who stole a bunch of Punk rock records from Goof friend Scary Mary and tried to sell them. During his "trial" he was given the choice of getting his hair cut off or his teeth kicked in. He made his choice. Scumbag jumped up in the air and elbow slammed the front of his face. They gave his teeth to Scary Mary who made earrings out of them.

None of the Goofs ever said no to a fight, and they didn't seem to be afraid of anybody. They say – unlike the Skinheads – they never fought as a gang and claim they never started fights or fought for the hell of it.

"I don't do backup. I'll march on 150 people, I don't give a fuck, that's like calling your mom or calling the cops," says Crazy Steve Goof. "If I need help I'll go get a brick. We stood and watched our friends get their heads kicked in because we didn't want to gang up. When you're a free agent like that, it's way more dangerous than a gang."

People were choked, hung, shackled, beaten, hit with frying pans and hatchets to the head and steel pipes to the face. Along the way fingers got sliced off, testicles were severed, faces were broken and many succumbed to the unfortunate force of gravity after being thrown off rooftops and down stairs. Shopping carts were used to rush people to the emergency room. Good thing it was only three blocks away.

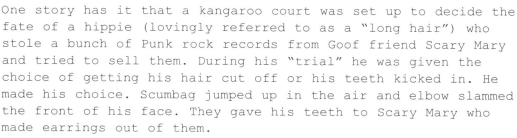

"WE WEREN'T

FONT NAME: IMPACT

PEACE PUNKS."

— CITIZEN GREG

8 5

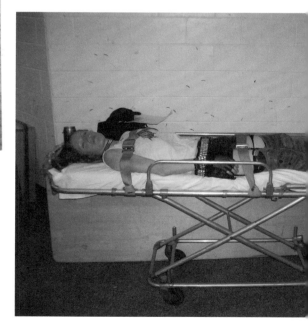

"We're not into crime. For a group of people to be classified as a gang, they have to be into crime. If there's no crime, there's no gang. There's nothing to be gained, so there's nothing to fight for."

— Crazy Steve Goof —

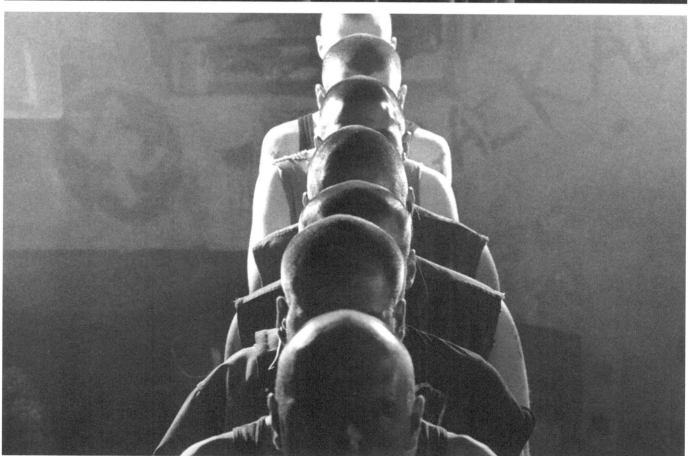

Photos by Miki Toma

FUCKING COMMIES SHOT THEM DOWN
FUCKING COMMIES KILLED THEM ALL
A FRIEND WAS ON THAT PLANE THAT DAY
FUCKING COMMIES BLEW THEM AWAY

KAL 007 MADE A MISTAKE AND WENT TO HEAVEN

WON'T GO TO HELL 4 THIER SINS

JUST THE COMMIES AND THIER KIN
START A WAR AS EASY AS THAT
DENY THE TRUTH FROM THE WORLD

DENY IT ALL - DON'T PAY A CENT - TO DEPENDANTS AND GOVERNMEN.
STANDARD PRACTICE ALL THE TIME
SHOOT THEM DOWN IF THEY STRAY THE LINE
PASSENGER PLANES R AN EASY MARK - PRACTICE TIL THE REAL WAR STARTS
ANDROPOV DIED - 2 MAKE US FORGET - ALL ABOUT THAT SILLY JET
HE WAS TO BLAME IS WHAT THEY'LL SAY - HE'S GONE NOW -
WON'T HAVE 2 PAY

FIGHTER PILOTS GLOAT AND BOAST
GOT ME A JET JUST OFF THE COAST
WRONG PLACE RIGHT TIME
YANKEE PLANES LOOK ALL THE SAME
RADAR BLIPS DONT TELL TO MUCH BUT
THEN AGAIN NO ONE DOES
PROTESTING TO THE UNITED NATION
BRINGS ABOUT ALLOT OF FRUSTRATION

ANDROPOV'S DEAD - BUT THINGS ARE THE SAME

BEEN DEAD 4 MONTHS BUT NOTHING CHANGED

ANDRODED INTO A BIG RED CHAIR - HE SIGNS THE PAPERS AND DOESN'T CARE

THEY'LL KEEP HIM THERE AS LONG AS THEY CAN
A ROBOT'S BAD BUT NOT AS A MAN
PROP HIM UP WITH SLIVERS OF WOOD
NO ONE WILL NOTICE - MAKE IT LOOK GOOD
U CAN'T GIVE IN COS U KNOW THE PLAN - CAN'T GIVE RUSSIA
TO THE CARDBOARD MAN.
TRUE - DOUBT TRUE DOUGH U'VE GOT WHAT U WANTED
RETIRE NOW COS ITS ALL BEEN STARTED -
START YOURSELF OFF SOMEWHERE NEW - WITH A BILLION
VOICES TO BACK UP U - U'LL BE IN THE KREMLIN.
IN WEEKS - GO RITE NOW POPULARITY PEEK
RONALD REAGAN PUSHING U IN - WELL ALL RITE SOMEONES
GOTTA RUN THINGS.   ELEVATOR MUSIC ON THE RADIO -
SOMEONES DEAD I CAN TELL - IGOR BACK FROM
STOCK HOUSE - DIMITRI STAYS AT HOME - FUELING
SPECULATION THATS BEEN GOING ON 4 MOTHS
ANDROP

KAL 007
LYRICS BY SCRAG

GO TO HELL 4 THIER SINS

THE COMMIES AND THIER KIN

A WAR AS EASY AS THAT

THE TRUTH FROM THE WORLD

T ALL - DON'T PAY A CENT - TO DEPENDANTS

OARD PRACTICE ALL THE TIME

T THEM DOWN IF THEY STRAY

R PLACES R AN EASY MARK - PRACTICE TIL THE REAL WA

OU DIED - 2 MAKE US FORGET - ALL ABOUT THAT

S TO BLAME IS WHAT THEY'LL SAY - HE'S GONE

HAVE 2 PAY

ATTER PILOTS GLOAT AND BO

T ME A JET JUST OFF THE CO

RONG PLACE RIGHT TIME

NKEE PLANES LOOK ALL THE

AD AR BLIPS DONT TELL TO MUC

EN AGAIN NO-ONE DOES

TESTING TO THE UNITED

RINGS ABOUT ALLOT OF FRUS

NS DEAD - BUT THINGS ARE THE SAME

DEAD 4 MONTHS BUT NOTHING CHANGED

ED INTO A BIG RED CHAIR - HE SIGNS THE PAPERS AND

KEEP HIM THERE AS LONG AS THEY CAN

OT'S BAD BUT NOT AS A MAN

HIM UP WITH SLIVERS OF WOOD

IN DOG
WE TRUST

THE DOGS WERE LIKE THEIR MASTERS…THEY LIKED TO FIGHT AND THEY LIKED TO FUCK.

IN DOG
WE TRU

Goof dogs were treated like gods and battle companions. Fists flew all the time at the Fort, but if you messed with the dogs you got your head kicked in. No one fucked with the dogs. If they got hurt so did you. People would get punched out for feeding the dogs booze. Or throwing lit cigarettes on the ground when the dogs were around. Broken glass in the Fort was unacceptable.

The dogs, like the Goofs, had a pack mentality. Dirt (aka Dirty, Berkley, Dirk, Dirdle, Turtle, Tartou) was Crazy Steve Goof's dog. Steve was the alpha male and Dirt was the alpha dog. Story goes he was part husky, part shepherd, part prison dog. Dirt was not a one-woman dog, and along with countless bitches produced somewhere around three dozen pups. Many of Dirt's sons and daughters went to fellow Goofs. It was a badge of honour to have a Dirt dog.

"I had two females, Berlin and Autumn. I brought them down to the Fort and then the next thing Dirt is slamming them all the time and puppies were coming out like crazy and I was giving puppies to all my friends. That's how all the dogs came about."
— *MadDog, master of Autumn and Berlin (two of Dirt's bitches)* —

"I loved Dirt. He never gave me a hard time, never ratted me out, never told the next girl to come in the room what was going on an hour earlier. He loved girl dogs and girls, and hated males. The only people he ever fucked up, fucked with him. He bit lots of people. One of the most famous BFG images, which we put on posters and t-shirts, is a drawing of Dirt with a dog bowl full of severed hands with one in his mouth. When Dirt came into a room he would nudge you to pat him, and as soon as you stopped he'd grab your hand in his mouth. People would come in to the room with their arms crossed."
— *Crazy Steve Goof, master of Dirt* —

"Everything at the Fort smelled like dog but that was understandable because there were at least half a dozen dogs living there at any given time. There was dog worship going on. The dogs were considered to be the social role model. It was really interesting how heavily they used dogs as the basis of their, you know, social cosmology."
— *Rick McGinnis* —

"Dirt was one of the first friends I ever made at the Fort. He and I got along. If anybody came near me that I didn't like, he would bite them."
— *Susana, painter of Dirt portrait* —

"They were good guards. If you're on a tour bus, you throw a couple of dogs in and no one would break in. Then when you go out to a show and seven dogs are in the Fort, who's going to walk into that? If anyone came in the backyard, the dogs would let you know right away. They were chained up and everyone would have to walk between them without much room to spare. One of the dogs liked to bite people's asses as they came in."
— *MadDog* —

"You would feed your dog before you would feed yourself. If you were broke and you had no money and you had just enough for a little bit of food, you'd get dog food 'cause your dog didn't have a choice in the matter. You could always go out and find another way of getting food. So your dog kind of came first."
— *Thor, master of Hammer* —

"Dirt travelled across the country in a tour van. He flew on planes and even went to Northern Newfoundland, Mexico and Guatemala. He was in movies; he was in plays. He even had birthday parties. Dirt died in Mexico in Zipolite (The Beach of the Dead) two months before his fifteenth birthday."
— *Crazy Steve Goof* —

Dirt's Wake, 1996

It says open ..but I
don't see anyone,Oh yes
there he is The

come on buddy
give the doggy
a bone...

or I won't let
you out of
your st ore.

shit whatever it
Oh it's liver,be
I kind of had m

mind set on pork.oops
droped it I hate get'n
pieces of butcher's

this guy looks
a little paranoid
he's not gonna
come out here.

Whats that
in his hand?

sawdust between my teeth
mmmmm tastes like more..*

DIRT SAYS...

I'LL TAKE A
HAND+CHEESE
SANDWICH, PLEASE

5

On May 5th, 2010, Crazy Steve Goof bought 55 lottery tickets from 55 different stores. It took him all day riding around the city on his bike. And it cost him $550 dollars.

The number 5 is considered magic, 555 not being anywhere near as bad as 666.

It all started with a guy named Burp. His real name was Vic, which starts with V - the Roman numeral for 5. He believed in a big philosophy, the three BPs: be positive, be polite and be prepared.

That's why he changed his name to Burp: UR surrounded by BP. Burp.

He believed that 5 was a base and the root of all power symbols. For example, if you take two number 5s and cross them on top of each other, it becomes a swastika.

Everything revolved around 5 for him. He even had a '55 Chevy.

"Burp was wild. On May 5th every year he'd go to the subway station and he'd wait until 5:55 and he'd try and get 55 transfers out of the machines. One time I had to go to court and it looked like he was going to jail and he had 55 transfers from May 5th at 5:55 in a bundle. He tore them in half and put a rubber band around each half. I put half in my pocket, he put half in his pocket and I got off." – Crazy Steve Goof

"He coated his walls in aluminum foil and wore the hat and said, "They're listening to us — the rays — and you should do your room. You're my brothers; I love you, I want to look after you. Come hide in my room." – Vic Victorious

Here's how the number "5" comes to play in Crazy Steve Goof's world…

• The band started when Steve was 25
• The band had 25 members
• The band made 5 real recordings
• Crazy Steve Goof's birthday is on the 15th
• Crazy Steve Goof left home at 15
• Dirt almost made it to 15
• The band ended when Crazy Steve Goof turned 50
• The first Fort at Baldwin lasted 5 years to the day
• The second Fort at Oxford died on May 5th
• The Bunchofuckingoofs last show was 25 years to the day after their first one.

Burp died from an aneurism probably caused by a baseball bat that had taken to the head years earlier.

B is the second letter of the alphabet
F is the sixth letter of the alphabet
G is the seventh letter of the alphabet

B=2
F=6
G=7
BFG=15

YOU WANT ME TO INCLUDE WHAT?

CHAPTER 100

"YOU HAVE
TO HAVE A
CHAPTER ON
STEVE'S COCK."

— KING KONG —

CRAZY

I like it better when I'm walking down the street and people are trying to attack me and are afraid of me and spit at me and call me names. It's better than being accepted. I never wanted to be accepted.

STEVE

GOOF

GON

CRAZY

STEVE

GOOF

Sunday SUN

TORONTO December 4, 1983

Punk rock singer Stephen Johnston, 25, wheeled his defence into court Friday — his bicycle.

He parked it by the jury box and then pleaded not guilty to a charge of possessing burglary tools.

He told Judge Arthur Whealy the tools, a screwdriver and vice-grip, were to fix his mode of transport, not commit burglary.

Johnson, of Baldwin St., was arrested May 3 outside a factory at Richmond and Spadina Aves., said Crown attorney Paul Layefsky.

Whealy said he'd never heard such a concoction of defence and Johnston was convicted.

He was put on probation for three years and ordered to do 22 hours community work each of the three years.

Whealy had a word to describe Johnston's bike as well, he called it a "wreck."

THE START OF CRAZY

My hatred for the system started early. I'm fifteen years old. I've been working. I get my tax return cheque: they won't cash it at the bank because I have insufficient ID cos I'm not old enough to get a credit card, because I'm not old enough to have a driver's licence, and I want to tear somebody's fucking head off. They wouldn't cash the fucking cheque, and right there I thought, this is completely fucked. That was when I first said, "fuck you" to the whole thing.

Back then, I was doing everything and anything. I was huffing nail polish remover. I was shooting speed in pool hall washrooms. I was doing B and E's. I was forging cheques. Glue, speed, coke, and heroin, whatever, I did 'em all. That's why I have such a strong opinion about hard drugs now.

I quit school at the end of Grade 8 and got a job. I had to go to court to get them to let me to get out of school. I was happy. I was making money. I wasn't dependent on my parents. They had me paying room and board when I was fifteen. So I wasn't going to listen to them. I'm paying my own way. I'm coming home when I want, bringing home who I want and doing what I want when I get there.

DOIN' DRUGS

I did coke for ten years before I became a crack addict. We all did coke when it first came around. I lived through drug abuse, many of my friends didn't. I've got a list of people in my computer that's at fifty-three right now. Fifty-three dead friends and most of them are from drugs. I don't go to junkies' funerals anymore. I don't celebrate stupidity.

PUNK IS . . .

Punk is not choreographed, pre-conceived bullshit. What isn't Punk? It's almost all not Punk. What makes Punk Punk is the reason why it happens. If the person's motivation for being in that band is just to be a rock star, then it's not Punk because it's not real. Punks don't just talk about it, they don't just put up posters, they don't just sing songs about it. They deal with it and that's what Punk is about. Punk is about anarchy. It's about self-responsibility. If you're a Punk you don't call the cops, you deal with it. That's Punk. Punk is not contributing to this disaster that we live in. Punk isn't about buying the newest, latest. Punk isn't about spending money on clothes. Now there's a phenomenon. The "out of the box" Punks that come from the suburbs right now look like people did in '77, but they probably spent $800 on their clothes at Le Château. That's not what it's about. It's about fun, sex, dogs, garbage, responsibility.

BEING A PUNK MEANS…

I like it better when I'm walking down the street and people are trying to attack me and are afraid of me and spit at me and call me names. It's better than being accepted. I never wanted to be accepted.

What am I fighting for? I'm fighting so that I can stand on the fucking street, drink a beer, smoke a joint and do whatever I want as long as I'm not hurting anybody. That's what I'm fighting for.

Racism is total bullshit. If you're going to say that you should hate everybody that's not white, that means you should love everybody that's white. I don't like all white people. I don't like most people.

EARNIN' A BUCK . . .

I did anything if I was paid ten dollars or more an hour to do it. I
did all kinds of stuff…setup for big, crappy bands at the SkyDome, I
was a doorman. I was Mr. Mover the last three days of every month. I
did construction, I dug holes… I lived in my truck for five and a half
years, not worrying about how I was gonna pay the bills. It was the
best move I ever made in my life. Total and absolute freedom. My last
place cost me $700 a month…I lived in poverty just so that I could
have a little bit of privacy.

Before the Goofs I had an antique store and then I got into real
estate for a while because the market was really good and I thought I
could make some fast money. I made $7,000 in the first six weeks and
then the market just fell apart. I was a Punk before I was into real
estate, though.

SEX AND THE SINGLE GUY . . .

I've never had a long-term girlfriend that I didn't cheat on in my
life.
     Two people get together they want to have a child… first, the woman
can't have sex for a while 'cause she's pregnant. Then there is a pair
of soggy, sloppy tits, then there's a fat ass, then there's some
stretch marks. Then there's no sex again for a while, then there this
whole change in priorities where the baby come first and the guy
doesn't matter and the friends don't matter and nothing that happened
before matters except for the baby. Then there's the idiot mother with
the baby who's spending a couple of years going goo goo gaa gaa, who
can never say anything intelligent ever again until she's thrown the
kid in nursery school and regained her brain by talking to adults
again. Then there's fifteen years of bullshit, money problems, aggrava-
tion, just so that some ungrateful little prick can turn around and
spit in your face after your life's over and it's too late and you've
wasted it.
     What kind of a fucking idiot would bring a child into this world
knowing that we're on the edge of ecological disaster…on the edge of
world war? Why would you do that? There's already too many people here
and most of them are a waste of oxygen, so why create more mindless
consumers to make more plastic to destroy more things, to care about
nothing but convenience and cash. What's the point?
     It's easy to have a relationship. What's difficult is to maintain
friendships.

     If you don't want to be lonely, get a dog. Dirt was the best com-
panion I ever had. He hung around with me for fifteen years, never
gave me a hard time, never questioned anything I did, never ratted me
out. Never told the next girl that came into my room what was going on
an hour earlier.
     I've survived rather well. I still drink every day and I smoke pot
every day and I fucking sleep wherever.
     Am I happy? I will be later when I'm getting my dick sucked. If
you don't like what is going on in your life you can just get up and
fucking walk away from any situation. If I'm not happy, I go for a
walk.

July 11, 1987

Mr. Steve Johnston
69 St. Andrew
Toronto, Ontario
M5T 1K7

Dear Mr. Johnston:

I am very scared of you.

I would like to have a meeting with you on Saturday July 18 regarding the upcoming event "Beer and Buddhism".

Specifically, to talk with yourself and Shawn about Pig Tumbler's part in this production.

I feel we need to discuss money, sound requirements, and scheduling.

I trust that you will find it possible to work with myself, even though I have the most totally negative outlook in the world.

Yours sincerely,

Andrew Heap

copy Shawn

PAGE 108...

LIVING IN THE NOW…

I'm not worried about the future because I don't really think there is that much of a future one way or another, I really don't. In 1983, we were talking about the end of the world because Reagan was all Alzheimered out and was about to push the button. But now we've got something even bigger and nastier on the go. If the world doesn't end soon it is just going to turn into some place you don't want to live. Dead and under the foot of the big guys.

There was no plan. There is no plan.

+++

TITLE: THE POSSE SPEAKS . . .
SUBTITLE: THESE FUCKERS SAID WHAT ABOUT ME?

"He's got some charm for an ugly motherfucker." Cretin

"He's a ladies' man, he's a fuckin' warrior and you got to earn that right, it's not a gift. Steve is one of those guys that will punch your face in and he will slam your fucking head on a table for being an asshole." John Tard

"If he directed himself in another way, he could have been a cult leader, no problem." Bruno

"Steve wouldn't have thought of himself as a leader. He was just the beer giver." Colleen Subasic

"He makes a lot of dudes want to have bigger balls and harder fists and all that shit, you know, but I've seen him help out a lot of people, a lot of people. As crazy as he is and as hard-ass as he is, he's done more good in this city than I've seen anybody do. So I got good props for that guy." Bones

"He's extremely charismatic, he's an excellent talker and he reads people really well and he's a very smart guy. He's just got these attitude problems. He's just full of his own ideas and thinks — it's kind of like George Bush — you're with him or you're against him." Colleen Subasic

"Steve's definitely smarter than the average bear and had a real knowledge of life because he's a bit older, quite a bit older actually, than a lot of the kids in the scene fresh out of the suburbs or from some small town somewhere. Steve was more in control than almost anybody around. Whereas, you know, some of these kids were just random particles, ricocheting off everyone. There was always this sense of things being on the verge of falling apart in that scene, but with Steve around it never really seemed that much of a threat. Rick McGinnis

"He's the reigning King of Kensington. Everybody understood what their role was in the Market, because it's their little fiefdom." Edward Mowbray

"To the street Punks of North America, Steve is worshipped like a god. You can see that in their eyes. He's telling them what they want to hear and they're all agreeing with it. He is the king of the street Punks. Cretin

"He's an unusual character. He's got charisma and he's very wedded to the character that he's built for himself as Mr. Steve Goof. I came to the whole Punk scene more through my art college background. And Steve could be civil at a gallery opening or completely uncivil at a Punk concert. He always encouraged people to be creative." Susana

"The Fort was a place where I was never made fun of or criticized and always treated with respect. When you're sixteen years old and trying to find where you fit in this godforsaken world, being accepted for who you are is half the battle. I showed up to my high school prom with Steve as my date. Coming from a tight-assed, all girls, Catholic high school, the look on the faces of teachers and students was priceless. On the drive down to the Boulevard Club, Steve was crammed into the trunk of my Mom's Toyota Corolla when he realized the zipper of the leather pants he borrowed from Merrick was busted. It was one fucking party I will never forget! And besides...who else would I have gotten my nickname from?" Sewage

"I was with Steve when we filmed *Millennium* out at the old Kodak factory. I remember they told extras they'd pay us $25 an hour more if we'd shave our heads. Steve seemed like a good guy, but the truth is he scared me. It was only after I got to know him a bit that I liked him. The whole Goof culture was odd because I think if they'd somehow been demystified, people wouldn't have been so quick to judge." Dave Bidini

"Do you know what a 'Super Male' is? That's like with your X and Y chromosomes...males are what two Ys and an X? Well, a super male is all Y chromosomes. I've got a suspicious feeling that Mr. Steve might be all Ys. He's a smart guy. He knows his wad. But you have to let the guy win every scenario because he is the Alpha Male. He's a born leader; he leads the people he's living around. There's lots of violence, but he had the best of intentions. He was bullying the bullies, with his own little militia if you could call them that. He's got very strong morals. He went and carved himself out a little kingdom there and he's been the true King of Kensington for the longest time. I've got no problem with his way. His is generally the right way. He treats people fair. He just lays down the law. He likes to have a steady flow of attractive young women around him too. The old man does quite well for himself." Cretin

Though MY PAL STEVE GOOF may have looked a bit frightening to some people (and not at all like anyone else) for the longest time, I wouldn't think of having a celebration at my home without wanting him there

Everyone was extra nice to one another when Steve was there.

Illustration by Erella 'Vent' Ganon

"For a while, every time I would bump into Crazy Steve, he'd be punching someone in the face. I'd see Steve after a Random Killing show, he would stop whatever he was doing to go punch Drew (Drool) the singer, in the face. He's a unique character who is a true Toronto Punk Rock legend. Whether it was being a squeegee 'pimp' as they called him during the squeegee corner disputes, keeping the streets Punk, or cleaning up messed up Punks. There is a heart there, and a devious smile. Most people would agree that you shouldn't give a microphone to Steve Goof when there are technical difficulties, cos he will start telling stories, about 'back in the day' at the Greeks, about how life was easier. Steve would go into these rants that would go on for hours, late into the night, delaying shows and pissing off bar owners. Anyone else would have had their mic turned off. No matter what he said, his fans would listen and let him finish. Sometimes there were ten kids left in the audience…other times hundreds. Either way the younger generation of punks saw Steve as a mentor." Rosina, aka The Frygirl

"I got beat up really bad at Brock and Queen when I was nineteen. I was told that some of the Goofs would go hang out where it happened, fishing for bullies. I don't condone violence, but the gesture was more touching than flowers. Steve, if you're reading this, thanks for visiting me at Sick Kids when I had that operation. And I'm still sorry Ruston, McCullough and I drank your beer at the Ramones show in Bala. We were really fucked up. Now we're even for all the times I got pieces of TV sets in my eyes, ears etc. One day Steve and Dirt were staying where I was living but I didn't know it. I went into the pitch-black back room to get a beer and stepped on Dirt. He barked like crazy and went at my pant leg but didn't bite me. My screaming and his barking went on for about two minutes of real time and he finally let me leave, humiliated and frantic, but not bleeding. That was really good of him. A true gentleman, or whatever." Dallas Good

"I lived on Augusta in the Market for thirteen years, and during that time the BFGs were a very visible presence in the 'hood. I wrote a funny little song about the shops and characters and the BFGs get a shout out. Back then, my obsession with Burt Bacharach kept me apart from the Punk world. But one scene that stands out in my mind happened outside Theatre Passe Muraille after a play about Queen West and The Cameron. Steve Goof was in a heated conflict with some fairly normal looking dude, and the tension was super scary. The normal guy just stood his ground and stared straight at Steve, and Steve looked crazed with anger and was all 'I know seven ways to take you down, mutherfucker!' From witnessing that I drew the conclusion that he was a bona fide Punk, and one should never fuck with him!" Kurt Swinghammer

"To be honest, I don't understand what the nostalgia's about. I have fond memories of Steve, who despite his heralded – and feigned – piss and vinegar stance was actually very gallant, a sort of outlaw gentleman, who kept quite a sweet eye out for me when I was a thirteen-year-old runaway. But, it was what it was, a bunch of drunk Punks. And, yes, dirty too. Very. I don't recall it with any sentimentality. As to the 'no drugs' bit, that was certainly Steve's view— but the rest of us were out of our fucking minds. PCP, MDA, smack, whatever we could get our hands on ... it wasn't elegant. When I said Steve's stance was feigned I didn't mean fake. I meant that, while he had this character he played – hard, rough Steve, leader of the gang! – he had a very sweet side as well. Maybe only the girls got to see that. I never saw him be rude to a woman; he had an extremely ingrained, if unusual, sense of right and wrong, and chivalry was certainly part of that. I always wondered where he came from, he was vague about his past and his family, but I thought he must have been somewhere decent. Despite the mayhem Cult of Personality existence he chose for himself, his values were solid and he was smart and very articulate. That set him apart from most of his dogged 'followers' who were mainly just a lot of lost, white trash, living crazy in the big smoke. I think where he came from and how he got there is more interesting than the whole phantasmagoria he spawned. What happened that makes a man like that want to live like that—for years. It's the kind of lifestyle that's supposed to be a wild phase, not your life. Well, not your life if you're as smart and charming as Steve was. It's as if he got lost in his own fantasy or addicted to the adulation of his mad dog acolytes. He could have done anything else and done it well." Anonymous

"He was kind of like my dad in a way." Drool

+++

CRAZY STEVE GOOF IS QUESTIONED . . . BUT THIS TIME, NOT BY THE COPS

Born: A long time ago on the Ides of March, six blocks from Kensington Market

Height, in combat boots: Six feet

Weight, in leathers: 160 lbs

Siblings: "No one else's business"

Family Heritage: Jamaican-Scottish

Disposition: Ugly

Favourite Market Food: Pussy

Favourite Beer(s): Czech, Polish and German

Longest Lasting Relationship: Fifteen years with Dirt

Body Art: Multiple scars

Favourite Non-Goof Band: All bands that aren't in it for the money

Flatscreen Or LCD: Either one smashed to pieces

Favourite Quote: Mine: "When it's way too late, you'll just be starting to understand"

Favourite Book: Criminal Code of Canada

Cigarettes Or Pot: Hash

Favourite Virtue: Knowing when to shut my mouth

Favourite Qualities in a Man: Being able to know when to keep his mouth shut

Favourite Qualities in a Woman: Being able to know when to keep her mouth shut, and when to open it

Main Fault: Opening my mouth when I knew I should keep it shut

Idea of Happiness: Beer, fun, girls

Idea of Misery: Jail

Favourite Film: Road Warrior

Would Like To Live: On the street, everywhere

Present State of Mind: Completely insane

How I Wish To Die: Very messy

Talent I wish I had is . . . sucking my own dick

Personal Motto: Try me

Favourite Activities: Sex, drinking, patting dogs and trying everything once

Political Persuasion: Bucking and fucking the system

Best Decision: Cutting my hair

Biggest Fear: Fear

Number of Women Slept With: Working toward 3000 at the moment and getting real close

Blonde, Brunette Or Redhead: It's not what's on the top of her head, it's what's on the inside . . . but I like green a lot

Re-occurring Nightmare: Waking up fat and bald in the 'burbs

++

CRAZY STEVE GOOF'S INJURIES & INCARCERATIONS
For a ridiculously detailed list see www.dirtydrunkandpunk.com

Broke ribs flipping car into farmer's field.

Broke hands and toes "a bunch" of times punching and kicking people.

Tore ligament in big toe jumping off the eight-foot stage in bare feet at the second Punkfest.

Broke nose (just once) in 1973.

Broke cheekbones after starting a fight with "coked-out" jocks after a show.

Ran home before last call to take Dirt out for a leak. Slipped on ice. Broke leg.

Threw a fake roundhouse at a friend's head. Snapped the kick back so he wouldn't hit him. Was standing on wet leaves. Broke leg again.

Fell off roof high on glue, separated shoulder.

Stabbed - as a joke - in the back.

Incarcerated in the Don Jail for two home invasions and beating up Skinheads Dango and Biff.

Shot three times with a pellet gun by Skinheads during a show.

Charged with "Weapons Dangerous" after cops found a studded leather bracelet under the bed he was in with a naked girl.

Arrested for having what police called "burglary tools" which included vice-grips, a mini-screwdriver and a glove.

Some interview excerpts taken from:
Not Dead Yet and *Punk X* by Edward Mowbray
Courtesy Not Dead Yet & Victory Video Arts © 1984

BUNCHOFUCKINGOOFS
FROM MONTREAL
NORTHERN VULTURES
RANDOM KILLING
AND... EGO WHIP

WE'RE BACK

AT THE '66 APOCALYPSE CLUB

WATCH THE MARVELOUS MERICK PLAY BASE AND COOK CHILI! WOW

FRIDAY MARCH 2ND.

$5 AT THE DOOR

SEE THE AMAZING AL PLAY GUITAR AND DO SOUND AT THE SAME TIME!!

YOU JUST WANT YOUR
MOMMY.

YOU JUST WANT TO BE A DAD SO THERE IS ALWAYS A MOM IN YOUR LIFE
USE CHILDREN AS THE CHAINS SO YOU DON'T LOSE YOUR WIFE
MEALS ALWAYS COOKED ON TIME AND LAUNDRY NEATLY STACKED
YOU THINK THAT COS YOU PAY THE BILLS SLAVERY'S BEEN BROUGHT BACK

NOW HER LIFE IS YOURS, COS YOU NEVER LIKED ALL OF HER FRIENDS
FOR ANY KIND OF COMPANIONSHIP IT'S ON YOU THAT SHE'LL HAVE TO DEPEND
CONSTANTLY SEEKING YOUR ATTENTION BY CATERING TO ALL YOUR WHIMS
NEVER GETTING ANYTHING IN RETURN ALWAYS WAITING FOR YOU TO BEGIN

YOUR PATHETIC LIFE'S NOT COMPLETE TIL YOU'VE PASSED ON THE FAMILY NAME
YOU KNOW YOUR PRECIOUS BLOODLINE IS OF YOU ALL THAT WILL REMAIN
YOU WANT YOUR PRECIOUS SON TO HAVE EVERYTHING YOU DIDN'T
NEVER TEACHING HIM RESPONSIBILITY ONLY FOOLISH GAMES AND DEPENDENCE

YOU'D KNOW HOW TO USE A SHOP-VAC —IN A SHOP
YOU SUDDENLY FORGET HOW AT THE CARPET — AND STOP
YOU UNDERSTAND SOAP AND WATER WHEN YOU ARE CLEANING — YOUR CAR
DIRTY POTS AND LAUNDRY ARE A MYSTERY — SO FAR
YOU KNOW HOW TO DRINK AND HAVE A GOOD TIME
ONLY ON BOY'S NIGHT OUT IS EVERYTHING FINE
AND YOU KNOW HOW TO HAVE SEX, THREE-STROKE CONVENIENCE FOR YOU
YOU DIDN'T NOTICE ANYONE ELSE THERE DURING YOUR MASTURBATORY SCREW

THE WHOLE IDEA'S COMPLETELY FUCKED UP AND TOTALLY OUTDATED
BUT YOU'LL PROBABLY CATCH SOME SUCKER IF YOUR HOOK IS PROPERLY BAITED
IF THIS IS THE TRAP YOU'VE PLANNED AS YOUR MOST IMPORTANT GOAL
MAKE SURE YOU'RE UP TO DOING YOUR SHARE YOU USELESS FUCKING ASSHOLE

ANOTHER STORY
THAT DOESN'T NEED SET DRESSING

THE SHOW at The Bridge on Bloor Street was boisterous and wild. The Painkillers opened the show, but the Punks from Buffalo failed to make an impact, unlike the Bunchofuckingoofs who tore the place apart. A muscular BFG associate named Thor was supposed to provide security, but instead the crazy Punk was responsible for much of the mayhem. With his twelve-inch mohawk and steel-capped boots, Thor appeared to be seven feet tall. The maniac proceeded to smash a TV set to bits onstage while the BFG played, accidentally hitting a careless fan in the face with an iron bar. Bodies and bottles flew through the air, and the dance floor was slick with blood. The fans were fired up and ready for action.

Then the DayGlo Abortions hit the stage.

Afterwards, almost everyone went to the party at Fort Goof. The building, in fact, was a 24/7 booze can, and the BFG always had beer for sale. Tucked away in a dark corner of Kensington Market, the party at Fort Goof never ended, and neither did a bloody war between a gang of glue-sniffing Nazi Skinheads and the BFG. This was a whole new world for the DayGlos, who had never seen anything quite like Fort Goof and its warlike inhabitants. "That was a very interesting place," says Rancid Randy, who arrived later to help drive Myrtle. "The Bunchofuckingoofs had steel cages around their beds, for chrissakes. That place was amazing." Crazy Steve Goof explains the cages: "Me and MadDog, the drummer, both had cages around our beds. I still do. The cages were to keep insane drunk chicks out, cos when you live in a booze can, you almost always wake up with some strange chick in your bed. Too often, you never got into bed with them but just woke up with them, not having a clue how they got there." Doesn't everyone have that problem?

Overrun with large attack dogs and covered with spray paint, Fort Goof was like a movie set for a documentary about Punk rockers, except everything and everyone was real. Though they were anything but strangers to Punk culture, the DayGlo Abortions were impressed with the fortress-like structure and its hardcore inhabitants. "It was quite the eye-opening experience," reiterates Randy. The BFG were very accommodating and allowed Mike to drink as much beer as he wanted, which was plenty. "I immediately fell in love with their scene," says Mike Anus. "I thought it was great—it was like hardcore heaven." What they didn't tell Mike was that he was running a tab he'd have to pay back later. How the guitarist was able to cover the tab remains unclear, but he didn't just walk away from it. "Mike just went overboard, he was having too much fun," laughs Rancid Randy. Steve Goof doesn't recall the exact figure: "Like everyone that stayed there, Mike ended up with some astronomical beer tab. He probably had to pay me back with money from several welfare cheques."

From *Argh Fuck Kill: The Story of the DayGlo Abortions*
By Chris Walter
www.punkbooks.com

"I scream in front of a bunch of fucking retards!"
Crazy Steve Goof

CLOSE ENCOUNTERS OF THE PUNK KIND

THEIR DAY JOB WAS TO PLAY MUSIC AND
SCARE THE SHIT OUT OF PEOPLE!

PEOPLE
CAME TO SEE THE BFGS FOR
THEIR MUSIC AS MUCH AS FOR THE ON-
STAGE CIRCUS. THEY WERE THE EPITOME OF A
BEER BAND. BAR OWNERS LOVED THEM BECAUSE
THEY SOLD SO MUCH BEER.

"IF YOU DON'T SELL BEER, YOU MIGHT AS WELL BE PLAYING A
FUCKING PARKING LOT," SAYS CARSON T. FOSTER WHO BOOKED
ALL THE BANDS AT TORONTO'S RIVOLI CLUB, INCLUDING THE GOOFS A
BUNCH OF TIMES. "THEY NEVER DRANK LIQUOR, ONLY CANADIAN
BEER."

"OUR CROWD DRINKS AND DRINKS AND DRINKS," SAYS CRAZY STEVE
GOOF. "THE BAR OWNERS JUST SIT THERE AND SHAKE THEIR FUCKING
HEADS BECAUSE THEY CAN'T BELIEVE THAT WE INCITE SO MUCH SERIOUS
ALCOHOLISM."

WITH THE EXCEPTION OF ONE NEW YEAR'S EVE AT THE DMZ, THE GOOFS
HAD A REPUTATION FOR CLEANING UP AFTER THEMSELVES. LEAVE NO
TRACE BEHIND [RULE #5]. LIKE GOOD BOY AND GIRL SCOUTS, THEY
LOOKED AFTER THE PLACES THEY PLAYED.

BANDS MOVED IN PACKS, OPENING AT EACH OTHER'S SHOWS,
THEIR AUDIENCE TAGGING ALONG, FOLLOWING A TRAIL OF
POSTERS STAPLED ONTO WOODEN TELEPHONE POLES,
PHOTOCOPIED FLYERS HANDED OUT AT ONE
SHOW PROMOTING THE NEXT, OR GOOD
OLD-FASHIONED WORD OF
MOUTH.

. . . . .
. . . .
. . .
. .
.
.

PLAYING IN THE DE-MILITARIZED ZONE

Crazy Steve Goof says that, like everything else in the lives of the Goofs, the DMZ was dropped into their hands. The first DMZ opened in 1985, where the Spadina liquor store is now, just above Dundas. Originally called the Paramount, it was one of the first Toronto bars to have a metal detector.

They took over the Paramount and turned it into a Punk music palace. It was the only club the Goofs ever owned or operated. Burp came up with the name. This no man's land of Punk rock held around 300, was open seven days a week, and cost a buck a band to get in if the Goofs booked the band, a bit more if a promoter booked in bands from out of town.

Dogs were welcome during the day, but it was too loud for them to be there at night. Naturally, the place got busted for underage drinking and for people drinking outside the club. Bands like Agnostic Front, House of Commons, The Freeze and Batallion of Saints played alongside the Goofs.

The second DMZ was above Blondie's on Dovercourt Avenue in early '86. Blondie's was allegedly a mob run disco that was rumoured to hire its staff fresh out of jail. The same shit went on there as the first DMZ (insert crazy, drunken stories here...) Steve and the owner hated each other, because, in Crazy Steve Goof's words, "He was a douchebag and I was not." Needless to say, the end was apocalyptic. Here's an excerpt from *NOW Magazine*:

"Apparently the proprietors became convinced the concept was unviable when, on New Year's Eve, a few patrons, incensed with the holiday spirit, decided to trash the women's washroom. The owners came in the following day and found much of the former washroom in the business office and told operator and booking manager Steve Johnston [sic] to take his customers elsewhere. No word is available as yet as to whether or not Johnston will seek to establish another DMZ elsewhere."

THE GREEKS

The Greeks was a tiny bar sandwiched between a fishmonger and an army surplus store on Baldwin Street in Kensington Market. Johnny the Greek ran it with his wife and sons. The outside patio could fit no more than a few tables, but often saw a dozen or more Punks and Market regulars hanging out on it. Inside wasn't that much bigger. You'd have to squeeze past the band to get to the washrooms downstairs.

The place was always full of oddballs: Rochdale hippie types, street people, Punks, Rastas and people looking for cheap, late night beer or a really good gyro.

Back in the day it was the only place in the Market open after five in the evening. Except for the Greeks, the Market was deserted. Johnny fed most of the Goofs and let them hang out day and night — dogs included.

Bottled beer was the cheapest in town: $2.50 and the home-cooked food was delicious. "Johnny kept that place around literally for the entertainment value," believes Crazy Steve Goof. "He let us run tabs. Why would you do that? From a business point of view it's a terrible idea." The Goofs did their best to honour them, but often couldn't pay up and would end up doing odd jobs like painting for him.

The Goofs loved Johnny and Johnny loved the Goofs. The Greeks was like a second clubhouse to the Goofs and their Punk entourage. When fights would break out, as long as his place wasn't getting wrecked, Johnny the Greek would just laugh his ass off and tell them to take it outside. He never shouted at people unless things got really out of hand.

Thor, who worked as a bouncer at the Greeks, remembers making a best friend there while on the job. "One day I asked Johnny if I could get dinner on a tab. Merrick was sitting on the patio outside. Johnny says, 'You want dinner, you go punch him in the head, I give you free dinner.' I'm like, all right. Merrick owed Johnny a hefty tab and hadn't been around for a while. Johnny was not happy. So I walked outside and asked, 'Are you Merrick?' He said yes and I cracked him in the face. Merrick said, 'What the fuck?' And I told him Johnny offered me free dinner to punch you in the head 'cause you owe him money on your tab. Merrick was totally cool about it. That's how me and Merrick met and we instantly became friends."

57 CHANNELS AND NOTHING ON

"As far as I'm concerned, TV is worse than tobacco, alcohol and all that shit," rants Crazy Steve Goof. He wrote the song "Pre-Programmed" [see page 75] to commemorate his hate-on. No one watched TV at the Fort till the 90's when they hooked one up to a VCR to watch movies and porn.

If you brought a TV to a BFG show, you got in free. Destroying them became part of their stage show. At first they kept the TVs plugged in but soon realized that spilt beer and crowbars made the threat of electrocution not much fun. They would end their shows with "Pre-Programmed," and destroyed the

THIS IS THE UPCOMING D.M.Z. LINEUP TO DATE:

CONTACT CRAZY STEVE::: RESIDENCE 593-6871
DMZ 596-8880
PAGER 589-3446 (LEAVE MESSAGE AT TONE)

I WILL INFORM YOU OF ANY CHANGES BY PHONE

MAY 17   GROOVY RELIGION
          A NEON ROME
          BIG KING CORPSE
MAY 18   MATINEE   SATAN COUNTRY
          NITE   GARBAGEMEN
MAY 20   CLOSED
MAY 21   ANIMAL STAGS
MAY 22   BUNCHOFUCKINGOOFS
MAY 23   ARTSECT
          ABSOLUTE WHORES
          MR. SCIENCE
MAY 24   BATTALION $$ OF SAINTS (SAN FRANCISCO)
          CHRONIC SUBMISSION
          TERMINAL RAGE
MAY 25   MAJOR ADEPT (BUFFALO)
          PAINKILLERS (BUFFALO)
MAY 27
    28   TORONTO HARDCORE VIDEOS
    29
MAY 30   THIRD MAN IN
          BUDDY LOVE
MAY 31   SUDDEN IMPACT
          TERMINAL RAGE
          SLAUGHTER
JUNE 1   DEADBEAT
          NORDA
JUNE 4   FEEDBACK FEST 85
JUNE 5   HAPPY WORLD (DENVER)
JUNE 6   NATHAN BERMAN
JUNE 7   ALTA MODA (FIRST GIG OF TOUR)
JUNE 8   THE ENIGMAS (VANCOUVER)
          NO MEANS NO)VICTORIA(
JUNE 13   NO MEANS NO (VICTORIA)
JUNE 14   SECTION 8
          MONSTERS
JUNE 21   SON OF SAM (DETROIT)
JUNE 22   MAD SPRAY PAINT ARTIST OF QUEEN STREET BENEFIT
          BBBBB$E$$$
          BUNCHOFUCKINGOOFS
          CHRONIC SUBMISSION
          ANIMAL STAGS
          DIRECT ACTION
          NORDA
          BLIBBER AND THE RAT CRUSHERS
          HYPE
          AND MORE TO BE ANNOUNCED
JUNE 26   PEOPLE WILL TALK (BRANTFORD)
JUNE 27   STARK RAVING MAD (AMERICAN)
JUNE 28   THE FREEZE (BOSTON)
          76% UNCERTAIN (CONN.)
          HYPE
          NEGATIVE GAIN
JUNE 29   DIRECT ACTION
JULY 2   VAMPIRE $$$B$$$ LEZBOS (AMERICAN)
JULY 4   THE DUNDRELLS_ THOUGHT ROCKETS_ SUBTERRANEANS
JULY 5   NEGATIVE GAIN_
JULY 6   RAW POWER (ITALY)_ THE BREAKOUTS (S.F.)_ DIRECT ACTION

The second attempt at making the city safe for a **DMZ** club has ended with the demise of the club above **Blondie's** on Dovercourt. Apparently the proprieters became convinced the concept was unviable when, on New Year's Eve, a few patrons, incensed with the holiday spirit, decided to trash the women's washroom. The owners came in the following day and found much of the former washroom in the business office and told operator and booking manager **Steve Johnston** to take his customers elsewhere. No word is available as yet as to whether or not Johnston will seek to establish another DMZ elsewhere.

THE GREEKS

TVs during the song. At one show in Vancouver, they smashed two dozen TVs in one night. They had arrived in the back of a van as a gift. Others were ripped from ceilings and walls in the bar. They were thrown in the pit along with leather couch cushions. "By the time we left the place was completely destroyed," says Bones. "It was one of the most beautiful things I've ever seen in my fucking life."

As they kicked, hammered and sometimes punched the TVs into smithereens, microscopic glass fragments flew all over the place, all over the band and into the crowd. The glassy dust ended up scratching Scumbag's corneas. MadDog remembers their eyes feeling like sandpaper, not to mention the sensation of inhaling the toxic fumes that escaped. One guy blew out his ankle kicking a TV and Mopa Dean cut his hand to shit after punching one when he was drunk one night.

Some venue owners wouldn't let them play if they smashed the TVs. Others, like the Rivoli's Carson T. Foster, didn't care. "They'd roll out a carpet on stage before the show. And after the show they'd roll the broken bits up in it, and take it out." Sometimes the audience would grab brooms and help sweep up broken glass. At some point they stopped smashing TVs on stage. The glass and fumes became a serious health hazard. They just found other ways to hurt themselves.

SLAM-DANCING

Punks don't tango. They slam-dance. It was a contact sport set to music that looked a lot more violent then it was. In a way, it was a kind of collective, group dance. In a strange way, it's like "dancing" with other people. Bounding and rebounding off each other.

"Slam-dancing started out as fuckin' pogo kind of thing where everybody would jump up and down and fuckin' shoulder each other," says Crazy Steve Goof. "Then it turned into wrestling and then as the crowds got bigger and shows got bigger, then there was more stage-diving because obviously there were taller stages and bigger crowds to fuckin' climb on."

It was also about letting out aggression on the dance floor. People got taken down, but always helped back up. Yeah, some people got hurt. "There's a certain amount of bonding that comes across when you're a little bit trashed, and you just let it all let loose," says Mike Smallski. Vic Notorious, who worked as a doorman at The Turning Point, believed slam-dancing was an art form and would let the best slam-dancers in for free.

"There was this guy, Big Black Anthony, who nobody could ever knock off his feet, but I could always knock him on his ass and he hated that," says Bruno Bulldozer (who got the handles thanks to his prowess in the mosh pit). "One time he showed up in this leather vest covered in fish hooks and starts tearing up the dance floor. I still knocked him on his ass."

People would also stage-dive into the crowd, and sometimes ended up wiping out on a table or the floor if the crowd happened to part like the Red Sea at the wrong time. People were known to stage-dive off the fridge at the Fort.

Even girls got into the action. "I was about 120 pounds soaking wet, but pretty scary looking," says Jenny Snot. "One time, as I was heading into the pit, this guy looks at me and he says, 'You're not going to go in there, are you?' And I said, 'Yeah.' And he goes, 'You're going to get hurt. Girls always get hurt.' And I went, 'Fuck you.' So I jumped in and everybody's getting knocked around and then next thing you know, somebody grabs my boob. It was the guy who told me not to go in."

"Slam-dancing was a blast...the pounding, hard driving music just goes through you, letting it all out, going as hard as you want with your peers, throwing people on the ground, smashing people around," says Mike Smallski. "It's not like this anymore."

FIRE & BLOOD, THREE MORE EXAMPLES OF FUCKED-UP SHIT

Cisco lit himself and the stage on fire dozens of times. A few times he covered himself and the stage with lighter fluid and almost burned himself to a crisp. Once at the DMZ, he made a flashpot that had enough gunpowder in it for thirty flashes, and when he set it off a giant mushroom cloud blasted up and rolled across the ceiling sixty feet to the back wall, then down the wall to the bar. Everyone in the bar fled. The show was over.

In 2006, they played in front of 5000 hippies at the Marijuana March in Queen's Park. Afterwards, at the Kathedral, they burned a Confederate flag. It was twenty feet wide and stretched across the front of the stage. Moose came out in drag, wearing heels and a beard, and blew fire through the flag. It burst into flames and almost set all the speakers and lights on fire. Then the band broke into "Fascist Statement [see page 158]." The club was pissed.

At a show at the DMZ, the band tacked "squibs" (packs of fake blood used in movie gunshot scenes) against the back wall of the stage. A Goof in the audience jumped up, pretended he had a machine

128

gun and started spraying the stage and the band with "bullets." The squibs were rigged to explode thanks to a battery, wire and nails. It was an old-school props trick. And it worked.

WHAT HAPPENS IN COWTOWN, STAYS IN COWTOWN

"Our circus gives us everything we need. We go to towns and everybody comes and gives us exactly what we need. Women, beer and weed."
- Crazy Steve Goof

Once at a show in Calgary, this guy runs up onto the stage naked and gets on all fours, while his girlfriend shoves a full beer up his ass. Then he pulls the bottle out of his ass, takes a huge swig and smashes it over his head. King Kong pulls out a chainsaw – he liked to cut off the tops of beer bottles with it – tries to start it and nearly slices Crazy Steve Goof's cheek. Steve says, "Enough with the chainsaw." King Kong gets pissed and whips his pants down to his ankles. King Kong, like the rest of the band, has been on the road and hasn't showered or changed his clothes for weeks. The girl who shoved the beer bottle up her boyfriend's ass sees an opportunity with King Kong's exposed ass, crawls over and gives him a rim job. "That's the most disgusting thing I've ever done," she announces. No kidding.

FRENCH FRIED

"Once in Montreal after a show we played, we all took mushrooms and we went to a sex club. And just walking down the street it was like – I can't remember if it was a jazz festival or what but there were a lot of tourists around.

"I remember walking down the street with them, like both bands, BFGs and DayGlos," says Gymbo Jak. "So there was, like, a considerable, like fearful, amount of Punk rock walking down Sainte-Catherine. And I remember being stoned, looking around in people's faces going, well this is trippy, man. Look at these dudes I'm rollin' with, scariest dudes on the planet, you know. Especially Steve, he carries himself like a – walking around like a pit bull and everyone else is just like puppies, you know, poodles."

EYEWITNESS ACCOUNTS

FRONT MAN
"I saw them playing the Turning Point with Madhouse, I think it was around 1983. I was in Grade 9 or 10, had been going to these kinds of shows – nobody cared if you were underage back then – for the last year or so, but it was by far the worst violence I'd seen. Some guy at the show was causing trouble, screaming out for Led Zeppelin – kind of common at the time – and Steve grabbed a chain with a lock on the end of it, that was hanging out of the top pocket of his leather jacket and whaled this guy straight in the head. It was one fluid motion...his pocket must have been loaded with the chain specially for just such occasions." *- Craig Daniels*

THE NOTORIOUS BFGs
"I first heard of the band when I was in Grade 7. My friend runs up and shows me a ticket stub that read 'Bunchofuckingoofs.' We were later sent to detention for saying the name out loud in class. All I could think of was that one day I needed to see this band. In the mid to late 90's, the Goofs were playing places like the El Mocambo, 360, Lion's Club, Comfort Zone, Generator, as well as several after-hours clubs, jam spaces and several other seedy little places that would let them play. Most of the time it was for beer and a bit of cash (to buy more beer later).
"The first time I saw the Goofs was New Year's Eve, 1995 at the El Mocambo. The night was full of punk rock debauchery: moshing, slamming; Mohawks, swearing, fighting, studded leather jackets, lots of booze and a whole lot of chronic, which back in those days no one had a problem sparking up. Armed and Hammered and Random Killing were also playing that night. I woke up on Armed and Hammered's floor the next day." *- Rosina, aka Frygirl*

THERE'S NO LAW AGAINST CRAZY
"I saw one fucking idiot jump on a stage full of smashed TVs, slip and cut himself all over. Or this other guy who goes to kick a TV screen, blows his ankle out. TVs were hard to break. At Kathedral, another guy did the same thing...ran up to a pile of four or five TVs and did a super drop kick. For the next hour the guy was writhing in pain because his ankle was completely obliterated. You can't kick a TV out; it's not, like, paper-thin. Sometimes they had them turned on. They were all fuzzy." *- John Tard*

HEARING AID

"Once at the DMZ in the late 80s, my band, A Neon Rome, was doing soundcheck, and there was a question about whether or not one of the monitors was working. Godzilla – who was six feet tall with a six-inch Mohawk – came over and rather than put his ear down to the speaker, he picked the speaker up and brought it to his ear." - *John Borra*

BOOK 'EM

"I would much rather have booked a BFG show because even small incidents would have been policed – rather than a bunch of frat boys dancing to disco or hip-hop music. Those were always the troublesome shows from my perspective. Not the Goofs. You'd have to be a fool to go to a BFG show and start causing trouble. I'm not saying people never did it, but I never saw it." - *William New*

GOOD BROTHER

"I started a band when I was thirteen. It was 1986. My brother had been playing in bands for years, including Blibber and the Rat Crushers, so he used to listen to the Goofs. He loved them, that's why I started going to see them. After Steve's stint in politics, Kensington Market was like Haight-Ashbury. First time I went to the Fort, Steve welcomed me and my band inside. My dad loved the name Bunchofuckingoofs. Steve started calling the house, like, once a week, offering us shows. We were terrible and couldn't play on school nights but Steve's persistence got us gigs. At one point, we opened for 4.5 Reasons for a Retroactive Abortion and even recorded a couple of BFG covers. We were prepubescent skater kids from the suburbs, and we were awful. But Steve saw a band with potential and his support went above and beyond my own musical family and, because of him, I'm still making noise. And it's all his fault." - *Dallas Good*

IN PUNK WE TRUST

"I was given *Carnival of Chaos and Carnage* on cassette in my early teen years.

"I don't think any music or literature I owned at that point in my life could have prepared me for the strong and deliberate messages that the BFGs conveyed in such a threatening and hostile manner. The BFGs were aggressive, in your face, scary to say the least! Slamming in the pit and experiencing live the raw intensity of the BFG sound almost puts you in a punk rock trance of destruction which, in my opinion, is the only true way to experience the Goofs. Based on the crowd I would say that the Goofs had not only a following but a punk rock army. The Goofs didn't just play, they helped inspire countless local bands through their delivery of raw power and aggression." - *Christian Cannibal*

BAR BILL

"Renowned for their ability to render a club in ruins in four songs or less, the Goofs represent what many punk bands don't understand today; Extremity. 'There's something about smashing stuff that just gives you an adrenaline rush,' jests Steve Goof. 'Even if you can't hear the actual beer bottle smashing, you know you're destroying it, and it sends you into a frenzy.' After 18 years of El Kabong-ed guitars, broken glass, TV sets, club furniture and people, it would seem strange that the Goofs are one of the most highly respected bands on the Canadian circuit, with club owners begging for their return. But then one look at bar sales for a night of Goofy debauchery relates a different story." - *By Keith Carman / Chart Attack Magazine*

THE END?

A little bit of punk country

The eighth annual Punkfest was held in Marlbank (north of Napanee) on the weekend. One of the most p̶ ̶ ̶ ̶ ̶ ̶ ̶ ̶
festivals in Canada, the three-day event drew about 500 people. The festival was moved at the last minut̶ ̶ ̶ ̶ ̶ ̶mo-
ra (north of Belleville) after the municipality won an injunction against it, arguing its organizers' facilities ̶ ̶ ̶ ̶ ̶et
health and safety standards. Thirty b̶ ̶ ̶ ̶rformed, ̶ ̶ ̶ ̶ ̶potty Bot̶ ̶ ̶ ̶y Bird ̶ ̶ ̶ Po̶ ̶ ̶ and ̶

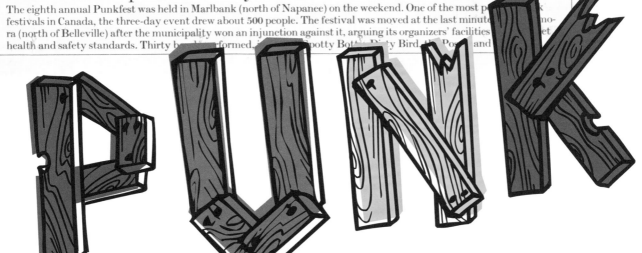

Punkfest was the brainchild of a guy named Spider. The first Punkfest, in July of 1991, was held, like all the others, on Spider's back porch on his eighty-acre piece of land in Marmora, Ontario, halfway between Toronto and Ottawa. The first Punkfest happened on Spider's birthday as a kind of massive party for himself. He was in his early fifties and although he was involved in London's R&B scene way long before Punk rock even existed, Spider dedicated his whole life to Punk rock.

Warren "Spider" Hastings was six-foot-five and often sported multicoloured hair, and sometimes a Mohawk. He drove a hearse, raised money for animal welfare and like Steve he was a kind of den-father to a sundry crew of hardcore and thrash-loving Punk rockers.

Punkfest was a three-day party, by Punks for Punks. There was no corporate sponsorship, there were no A&R music scouts there throwing

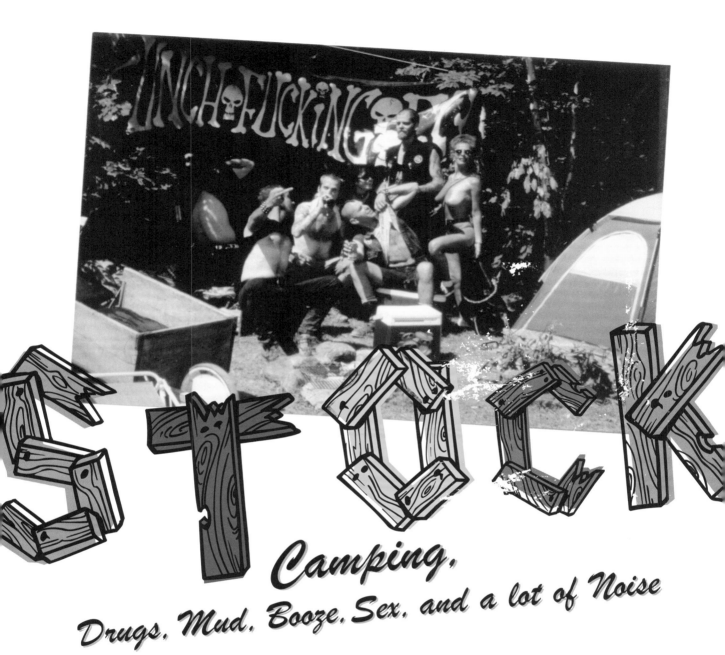

STOCK

Camping, Drugs, Mud, Booze, Sex, and a lot of Noise

record contracts at bands. Admission was around $20-30 for non-band members, but no one was ever refused, and most people never paid. Everyone camped, bringing their own food and alcohol.

Needless to say, there was never a shortage of beer. The Goofs took their booze can on the road, bringing with them as many as forty cases, with trips to the beer store to pick up forty more. They once bought two local stores completely out of Molson Ex. The Goofs would pack their van with so many cases of beer that they had to sit on top of it the whole way there.

The location helped create and unite the Punk scenes from Montreal to Toronto and all the small towns in between. Punks from all over the world would show up at Punkfest. The UK Subs played there, and of course the Goofs. The stages were small, and there was never any order to what bands went on when. It was a matter of finding the band whose members were the most sober, or weren't getting laid in the bushes, to come and play.

Punkfest grew from forty people watching and playing Punk rock on Spider's back porch to, at its peak, 4000 on a single weekend. Neighbours, the local city council and the cops weren't always happy with the festival.

There was also the occasional laser show and fireworks at night when the bands went on. One year they even had a midway with carnival rides.

The Goofs played every year except two, once playing a four-hour set until daybreak. Steve said Punkfest was the best party, with the best fights. The Goofs got in way too many fights. Spider hated violence.

The Restarts wrote a song called "The Pied Piper of Punk Rock,"

dedicated to Spider.

Tearin' down the main drag in the local village hearse,
Fighting back against stagnation and smashing the boredom curse,
He's a Punk rock one-man party and he's taking no prisoners,
Party all night 'til the early dawn, no time to be a pensioner.

Showed up on the local scene like a Fagin-esque Punk-queer bomb,
Age, race, or gender meant fuck-all, all that mattered was the party went on,

Uniting people from all walks of life and zero tolerance for bigotry,
Raise a glass to the man they called Spider and his Punk rock legacy.

Spider died in 2009 on Spiderland Acres. He was seventy-two. Some
people said he never looked a day over nineteen. "Spiderfest" contin-
ues: 2011 marks its twentieth anniversary.

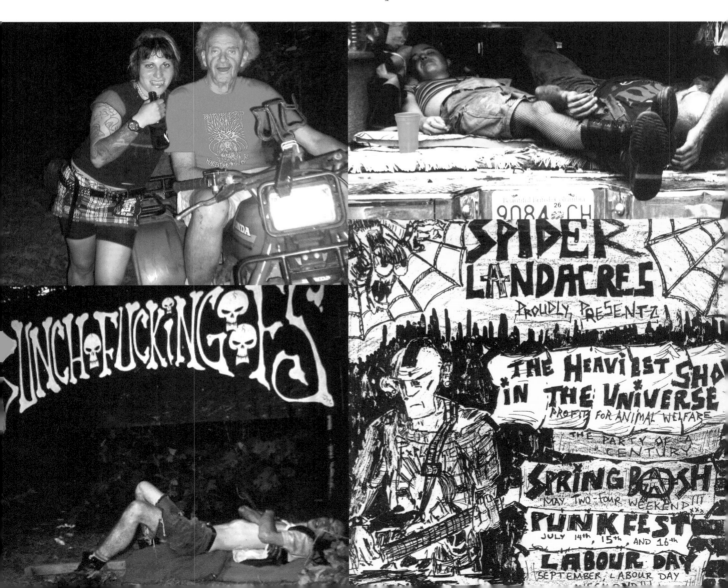

Beer, girls, music. That's what life is all about. Fuck cash, fuck music even.

– Crazy Steve Goof

the next night

the respite of this – the last physical bastion
of my private life. Same situation
as last night, but, god almighty,
more sober + enlightened, hideously,
once more.

– went out to Carol. BBull, Con-
met Greg – he snubbed us, which
was sad, in a pathetic way —
Sam w him, YAWN. hung out
w Scott B. + his laconic
pal, Dave. Finally, run into
Steve Goff, sometime friend +
Ptime sex god. he acknowledged
us. we drank more –
to two

LYNN CROSBIE'S FLASHBACKS ON CRAZY STEVE GOOF

"FORT GOOF" is a part of a poem sequence called Alphabet City (1998), a series of vignettes that take place in Toronto over the span of ten years or so. The poem speaks ardently to my wild love for Steve and my sense of the Goofs when I met them, as heroic, perfectly lethal outlaws.

"I've seen them come down on a guy like a plague of locusts," my friend Chris said, *sotto voce*, as we watched the Goofs pull up to the Cameron House one night in the late 1980s, looking for all the world like Mad Max and Knight Rider, apocalyptic dogs included.

I would later run into Steve as he and a friend broke into her locked car in the Market late one night. He told me how he used to work as a car salesman in a suit and when he forgot the keys he would slip a coat hanger surreptitiously from his pocket.

I noticed his beauty then also: big, ferocious black eyes with long, thick lashes; full lips; long, lean, strong body—he looked like Punk Elvis by way of a Latin matinee idol with a gangster past. I started hanging out at the Fort mostly to look at him. Steve was always in the eye of the hurricanes, composed but coiled up—it really was something to see him attack (when provoked): one felt the most beautiful sense of mortal terror.

Then again, I like danger, and Steve and I liked each other: most of the men I knew didn't enjoy the fear they felt when something was about to happen deep inside the volatile, snarling electrified confines of the Fort.

The Goofs were legendary by the time I met them, for their fast and frightening (and surpris-ingly funny, crazy-clever) music, their zero tolerance of junkies and psycho Skinheads (they ruled Kensington Market with a steel hand), and their booze cans that were harder to get into than the relatively tame Studio 54, in its own tempestuous heyday.

I spent my twenties working on my Ph.D and—among other wild exploits—drifting through the Fort till all hours in leopard negligees and spiked heels.

I was not the only misfit: the Fort was the place to get down and dirty, and I saw everyone who was anyone there in my time.

And it was, after all, where Steve lived. And slept in a cage with variations on the same maddeningly tall, blonde beautiful girl, or alone and watchful — a caged panther with a set of picklocks.

Meeting Steve was as close as a girl could come to meeting Lord Byron or Clint Eastwood's cowboy in *Unforgiven*, "meaner than William Bonney," but morally astute, and squarely, fundamentally good.

I remember my time with the Goofs as others remember, say, The Factory or Spahn Ranch (without the murders, naturally.) I am sorry to say to those who missed it that it can scarcely be described. You had to be there — breathless and sprawled on the roof among the metal trash, howling dogs; the ice-white light, and sweet summer heat and big, pulsing stars. It was heavenly.

Lynn Crosbie is a cultural critic, teacher, the author of six collections of poetry and two novels and a columnist for the Globe and Mail.

Top right: Crazy Steve Goof, Lynn Crosbie, Bruce McDonald, and Fraser Robinson; Bottom right: Lynn Crosbie's journal

voc-Te — he was obviously
marvous in his beauteous
resence. Went to ~~Fort Cook~~ —
like our 1st trip this week
re we were rudely ignored.
d the run of the dingiest
ce imaginable: and
- smells". Steve was
to me ~~[crossed out]~~ it
turn realized the full ex-
t of his animale magnetism.
one point, he spewed peach
napps into my mouth from
s own. We went outside
rapped. He + I

sat on the staircase — wch
one of the many drunired
black beasts. We talked,
+ when his friend arrived,
he, quite transcendently,
Kissed my face + we went
in. muchos amore ex-
changed + drunken —
" you can't come back w me"
etc.

So, all today, I was on the
hungover verge of "I love
him, truly". Went out w
Chris + Carol to the Cam.
+ was brought to earth.
Many men ogling Carol!

Feb 22/87

BRING ON THE PIGS

Meow . . . meow . . . meow . . .
I don't want a girlfriend
Just a fuck pig
Everyone's the same
What's it matter to you

If you think you're something
Put you in your place
Knees around your earholes
Pillow in your face

Bring on the pigs, come and go
Bring on the pigs, come and go
Bring on the pigs, come and go

I don't want a girlfriend
Just a fuck pig
Groupies by the nighttime
No relationships

If you think you're something
Put you in your place
Knees around your earholes
Pillow in your face

Degradation's your scene
You're a fuck pig

Bring on the pigs, come and go
Bring on the pigs, come and go
Bring on the pigs, come and go
Bring on the pigs, come and go

Just make us come and get the fuck out

Lyrics: Scrag and Crazy Steve Goof

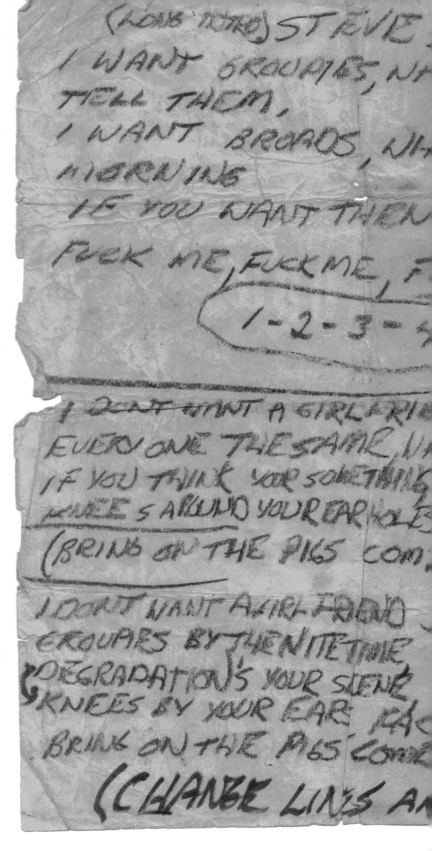

ME, FUCK ME
A F.P.
A F.P.

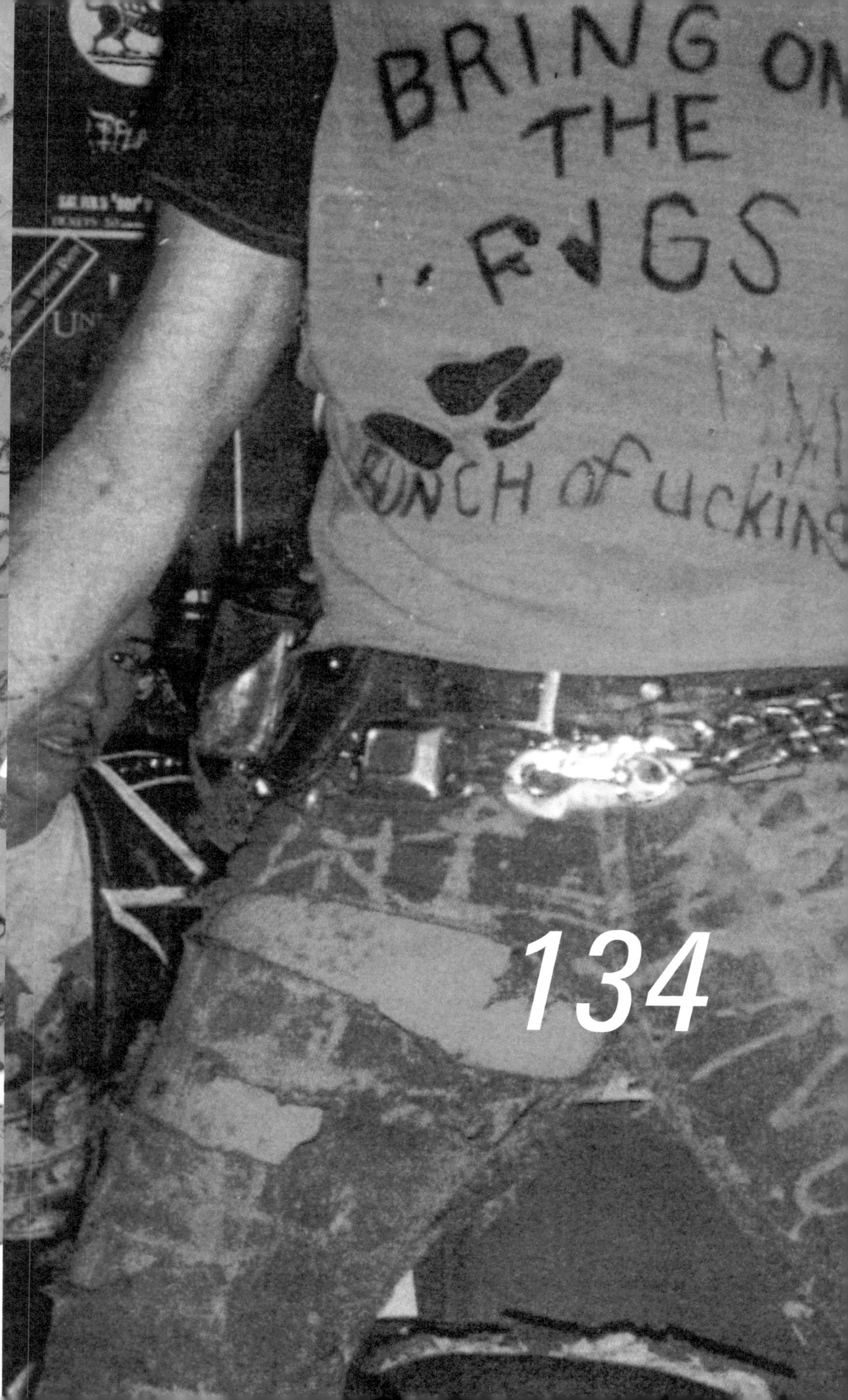
BRING ON
THE

NO
YOKOS
THEY PLAYED WITH THE BAND IN MORE WAYS THAN ONE

"The Punk rock girls were fucking scary, man. I guess in their minds they had something to prove cos they saw how tough their counterparts were and they were not to be fucking screwed with. And the best part was if you fucked around with one of them and the girl didn't beat the shit out of you or even if she did, the guys would beat the shit out of you right immediately after for being a jerk-off." – John Tard

"I was still a young woman in the '80s and there'd been lots of leaps forward for young women, but you still always got hit with a lot of conventional crap from men and society in general. But moving into the Punk thing, men no longer looked at me as being an attractive female; I was too freakish for them. And being involved in the whole Goof scene and the Market scene, even though I wasn't involved in the violent side of it, people still gave me a wide berth. I have to say by choosing the Punk subculture I eliminated a lot of the daily negative sexual attention young women got. The Punk thing left me free to move about the city and back then, most people moved out of our way, literally. Inside of that culture I developed an awareness of social justice issues and many of us were actively involved. Inside of that culture I developed sexual confidence and assertiveness, which was empowering." – Susana

"There were some guys there who turned out to be pretty good buddies but it wasn't on a sexual level. There was such a vast array of characters with crazy nicknames and crazy backgrounds. Once you got past the point of saying you're not going to sleep with them, that it wasn't a sexual thing, it was pretty cool. You could party with them and they would have your back." – Jenny Snot

"It was retarded. You wouldn't believe it. And the girls would brag – like me, a little young punk rocker, twenty-one, twenty-two, drag me into the bathroom, fuck me or blow me in the can and then leave me there with my pants around my ankles, and then go back into the show right. Wow. That was Punk rock." – Scumbag

"Everyone was having sex with everyone. We were young and primal. It was fun, not creepy." – Dawn Mourning

"Some of the chicks in that scene were really tough chicks." – Thor

"No one was put down because they were a girl or whatever. It was just no bed of wine and roses, that's all." – Scumbag

"I remember this one guy fucking around, grabbing chicks' asses and shit. All these guys wanted to kick the shit out of him. But this one girl goes, 'Let me do it' and she walked up to the guy, gave him a roundhouse kick right in the head and knocked him right to the fucking ground. I got beat up with a metal chair by a girl once, but you don't hit girls…you find another girl to beat her up for you." – MadDog

"Oh, the cum seeker. Man, she was awesome. She loved me, but she loved everybody else too. Remember Larry's Hideaway upstairs in the closet? Wow. What a champ. But in the band, that type of behaviour was more or less shunned because if you're heavily involved in a relationship with a girl or whatever, it's only going to tie you back from being able to do things, like pick up and go on tour for two months. The old lady's going to freak out or she's going to want to become Yoko Ono – come along and put her two cents in. So screw that crap. No Yokos." – Scumbag

"If you were having sex, you pretty much were having sex with everyone watching or hearing at the very least. It was just the way things were. Which brings to mind that whole commune thing. Not being a child of the 60's, I found it a little bit disconcerting. I never really wanted to live in those kinds of circumstances so I always found it kind of strange and a bit alien whenever I was [at the Fort]." – Rick McGinnis

"I was attached to Steve, so it was always pretty straight up, but I don't think any of the girls that ever stayed [at the Fort] ever had a difficult time, any more so than you would have staying anywhere with a bunch of guys. Sometimes they were complete slobs about stuff and they considered things like having no toilet paper a minor nuisance, but it was really pretty easy. Steve and I had had an on-again, off-again relationship over an eight-year period. We had a really good friendship in the off times. But there had been a crowd of girls before me that I used to jokingly refer to as 'the Fort pitbulls.' They were really keen on kind of establishing a hierarchy, and they were into starting physical fights with each other. But that really wasn't my scene at all." – Susana

147

148

150

"The social dynamic was that it was the girls that would hold down jobs and the guys who were always shuffling around from one shitty part-time job to another. It was the girls who would hold down steady, forty-hour-a-week positions and end up doing a lot of the financial heavy lifting." – Rick McGinnis

"There were two roles for women: girlfriends and fuck things. That's what they called themselves. The girlfriends were like holier than thou untouchables. The other women were just passed around. A lot of those girls came in just because they wanted to sort of be bad. They'd stay with somebody for a while and then move on to somebody else. I'm a girlfriend kind of guy, so I didn't go there. A lot of them were under age and I felt it was just wrong." – Vic Notorious

"There were a number of them on the scene that weren't terribly clever. But, they were there to wear the uniform and get some nice hard Punk cock. I mean that's really what they were there for and what they were about." – Edward Mowbray

"I was at a party once and this Punk guy, who thought he was Punker than thou, looked at me and he said, 'Oh, you're just one of those Goof chicks.' And I actually shoved him and stuck my heel in his groin and said, 'Say that again! I'm not just a Goof chick. I hang out with them, but I'm not owned by anybody.'" – Jenny Snot

"I'm glad I'm not doing that any more, but at the same time, I don't regret living like that, no." – Greenie

"The women were protected to a certain extent but certainly they were treated as chattel. We were called the fuck pigs. That's what girls were called. You're not going to get that part of the story from the guys." – TaraTaraTara

"And it even says on the first forty-five they put out, 'Thanks to all the fuck pigs!'" – Scrag

"Steve almost punched me out one night. Some girl was all over my boyfriend [Scumbag] and I told her to keep her hands off my boyfriend. She ran to Steve crying and said I kicked her out of the Fort. So Steve comes up to me and says, 'Do you want to be giving gum jobs for the rest of your life?' I'm only eighteen years old, and I'm sitting there shaking, thinking, 'What the hell is this all about? He wants to kill me?' So Scumbag takes him into the other room, they have a conversation, and then he comes out and says everything's okay. That's how women were treated. People don't like to talk about that part." – TaraTaraTara

"I remember watching this guy at the Fort grab this girl and start **fingerbanging** her in the washroom. I think his name was Stead. I had a fuckin' goofy disposable camera with me at the time . . . now you can just take photos of everything on your phone. The Fort was quite the party zone, I remember that. I remember how rad it was that everyone at the Fort had their own caged rooms, that they could just put a padlock on it and they'd be just like jail cells."

— Gymbo Jak

Dressed to kill in nothing
more than the shortest of skirts
limits of the imagination
Got one?
Eat your heart out sucker
It's hands off!
no fucking chance of fucking
A short skirt is not an invitation
It is a freedom
an insidious feminine power
wrapped up tight
and delivered neatly in motion
A most provocative deterrent
devastatingly effective in street warfare
And just how far can legs go?
It's your imagination
Got one?
It's all you'll get!
A barely decent facsimile of indecency
paraded in womanly terms
of confident stride and sexuality
guaranteed to annihilate
all but the coolest of gentlemen
with balls enough to appreciate
and cock enough to stay silent
Got one?

Poem by Dawn Mourning
From *Dressed to Kill*

"We're in the kitchen at the Fort, and there's a chick sitting on the counter touching the refrigerator. The refrigerator had no ground to it. So she's sitting on the counter touching the refrigerator and Crazy Steve Goof is grabbing the metal on the sink in the kitchen and creating this charge. He was sticking his tongue on her clit, electrocuting her. It was the most fucked up thing I'd ever seen in my life."

— Gymbo Jak

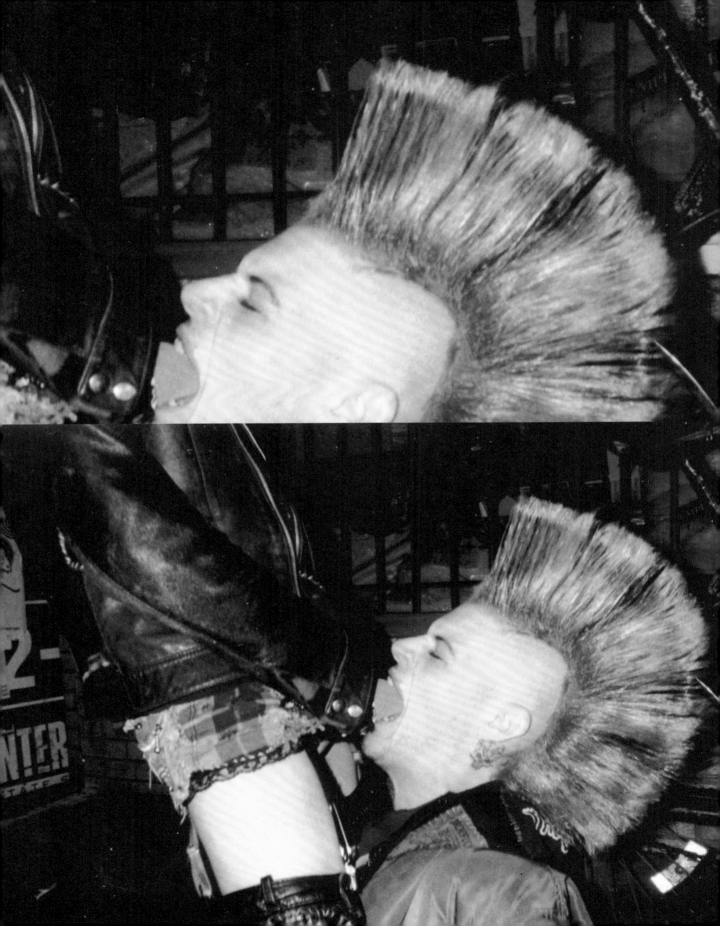

Goofs in Fiction

I GOT OFF AT SPADINA STATION. From there I hopped on a bus south to Kensington Market, near Chinatown. I got off at Dundas and went right into the streets of the Market until I found the alley I was looking for. It was behind a Vietnamese restaurant and a used clothing store that sold some really fuckin' cool red leather belts with three rows of studs in them. At the back of the alley was a stairway, one of those metal fire escape jobs. It went up to a second floor that used to be part of a warehouse. One window and a big metal door set in chipped red bricks. The stairway was covered in old bicycle parts, mostly chains and rims. Dogs, big German Shepherds, three of them, were tied up on the top level. All three had studded black leather collars that looked as if they had been ripped off the backs of the bikers in that Mad Max movie. They started barking when they saw me. I climbed to the top, and they started growling. I could see a little ways inside the door, but there was only darkness. I yelled out, "I want to talk to Steve! Is there anybody home?"

A voice yelled out, "Come in! Just walk by the dogs. They won't bite."

I walked past, and the dogs barked and growled as if they wanted to eat me. I stayed as far away from them as I could by hugging the railing and jumping through the door. Then I was in a beat-up kitchen. The yellow linoleum was worn out, and the fridge and walls were spray-painted with so much graffiti that it was too cluttered to read. Boxes of empty beer bottles took up a whole side of the room.

I walked through the door at the other end. It looked as if it had been a living room, but everything was spray-painted just like the kitchen. There was a big black Pearl drum kit with double bass drums in the middle of the floor. Against the walls, there were two huge stacks of Marshall amps and a mixing board. I could also see a couple of beat-up guitar cases covered in hardcore punk stickers, a red and black Fender Precision Bass, a blood coloured Gibson guitar and a microphone stand. I thought fuckin' eh! I'm in the practice spot of Sickness!

I knew it really was their space because Sickness was the only punk band that used double bass drums. Those drums made their music sound so driving and aggressive that you would think a truck was coming through the wall.

Real life punks have to live together to stay alive. They have to avoid so called 'normal' people. They have to tell those people to fuck off the second they start trying to tell them what clothes they should be wearing. I mean this was 1981 – there were what, a couple hundred punks in Toronto? There were hundreds of thousands of normalisms wearing the same fuckin' clothes and listening to the same fuckin' music in this city. There were billions of other mindless robot normalisms all round the world doing the same fuckin' thing. How the fuck is it that people like that can't put enough logic together to figure out that a few punks are not a threat to their way of life? How much of an asshole do you have to be to think you're fuckin' somebody special if you take a fuckin' unprovoked swing at an underdog?

The Terrible House of Sickness was the party palace I always dreamed of. I slept on the floor or sofa or anywhere the empty bottles hadn't piled up or the dogs weren't sleeping. Besides the guys in the band, Steve, Ringo, Crushed-Nuts and Bumper, I lived with a bunch of girls who were something like Sickness groupies. Those girls were always changing; one would move in one week and out the next. I remember the main girls. There was Bambi who was straggly like a rat, but always had her Mohawk soaped up so it stood in spikes. She always wore a dirty ballerina skirt under her long black leather jacket. There was Melanie with the rotten teeth who always wore dirty, torn sweaters kept together with huge safety pins. There was Regan who had long black hair and ten big silver skull rings on her fingers. She always dressed in black funeral dresses like Morticia from The Addams Family, and was so beautiful she could have been a model. There was Dog, who never said much, but was fat, had short hair and punched the walls a lot. I think she only had one pair of jeans and one t-shirt. Then, of course, there was me – Valerie.

Excerpted from *Spunky Punkette Seeks Romance and Adventure*
By Stewart Black
www.punkbooks.com

FASCIST STATEMENT

Hey there asshole
Mr. Fascist Statement
Nice boots you've got
Real nice braces
It looks to me like resistance mag's what you're reading
Looks to me like you need a real good fucking beating

I know it's not fair to judge a book by its cover
Prejudice is the problem but you look like the others
You wear the uniform of the sieg heiling masses
Why do you want to look like those heel-clicking assholes

The allies should have a look all of their own
So you feel your beliefs should be known
So why do you feel you can rely on just a patch
It's the only difference cos the uniforms match

If you take a strong stance you should make it real clear
A sniper's bullet knows no difference when the look is so near

The average idiot on the street cannot see the difference
The media won't help you so it doesn't make sense
And even though you're a trojan — you're still taking a chance
Cos all of you skinheads look the same at a glance

Of course you love the music cos ska is your life
But don't complain when you are stuck from behind with a knife

This isn't England and we know the skinhead's roots
They're supposed to look at the laces on your boots
But even in the scene no one agrees on the signs
Red — yellow — white laces and similar patch designs

And now that the gays and the b-boys are all dressing the same
Trendies and office clowns are all looking just as lame

Well for some it's all fashion
and for some it's their life
In three years you'll look different
don't lean back on that knife
Let them stand out
in any crowd that they're in
If we're not sure who they are
we won't know where to begin

So throw out that uniform
Or put it in a fire better yet
Dressing like the enemy
Is as stupid as it gets
Even on Halloween
You wouldn't dress like a cop
And even if you did
Tomorrow you would stop
Lose the image now before
You score someone else's shots
Bombers and braces
Cos you look real sweet in a pine box

It's so hard to tell the difference when they all look the same

159

𝕿𝕳𝕰 GOOF VERSUS SKINHEAD STREET WAR WENT ON FOR YEARS. BOTH GROUPS LISTENED TO PUNK MUSIC, RAGED AGAINST THE MACHINE AND PUT INDIVIDUAL FREEDOM BEFORE ANYTHING ELSE. AND THAT'S WHERE THE SIMILARITIES ENDED. THE LAST LINE OF "FASCIST STATEMENT" IS: "IT'S SO HARD TO TELL THE DIFFERENCE WHEN THEY ALL LOOK THE SAME." THERE WERE NEO-NAZI SKINS AS WELL AS ANTI-RACIST SKINS. BOTH HAD SHAVED HEADS, WORE POLISHED BOOTS, TIGHT JEANS, BRACES AND GREEN BOMBER JACKETS. PROBLEM WAS, YOU COULDN'T TELL THEM APART. AND THE GOOFS DIDN'T BOTHER TO.

161 HEADS

**I KNOW IT'S NOT FAIR TO JUDGE A BOOK BY ITS COVER
PREJUDICE IS THE PROBLEM BUT YOU LOOK LIKE THE OTHERS
YOU WEAR THE UNIFORM OF THE SIEG HEILING MASSES
WHY DO YOU WANT TO LOOK LIKE THOSE HEEL-CLICKING ASSHOLES**

"FASCIST STATEMENT," FROM <u>BARRAGE OF BATTERY AND BRUTALITY</u> [2000].

WEST END BOOT BOYS

THE TORONTO STAR
DEC 23, 1988

DEPUTY CHIEF WILLIAM MCCORMACK ESTIMATES METRO HAS ABOUT 300 SKINHEADS, MOST OF THEM IN THE DOWNTOWN AREA.

SKINHEAD GANGS ORIGINATED IN BRITAIN WHERE THEY WERE KNOW FOR THEIR OWN BRAND OF HOMOPHOBIC RIGHT-WING NATIONALISM.

+++

"BACK IN THE DAY THE TROJAN SKINS AND PUNKS USED TO HANG OUT TOGETHER. THEN YOU HAD YOUR NAZI SKINS WHO WERE NEO-NAZI ASSHOLES, THAT LATER BECAME A MOVEMENT ABOUT WHITE POWER AND THE KKK. THEY WERE WHITE SUPREMACIST BULLIES." — MOPA DEAN

"THE PUNKS USED TO HANG AROUND WITH THE SKINHEADS. WE ALL PARTIED TOGETHER; WE WERE ALL ONE GROUP. IT STARTED DIVERSIFYING WHEN WE GOT INTO A BAND AND THEY DIDN'T. ONE NIGHT THEY CAME BY THE FORT AND THEY TRASHED THE FORT, RAN HOLES THROUGH MY DRUMSKINS AND STOLE SOME SHIT. SO RIGHT FROM THERE THE SKIN WAR STARTED. IT WAS JUST A PARTICULAR GROUP OF SKINS AT THAT POINT, BUT WHEN ALL THOSE SKINS GOT EVERY OTHER SKIN INVOLVED, IT BECAME THE BFGS HATING THE SKINS AND SKINS HATING THE BFGS. IT WAS THE BFGS AGAINST A HALF A DOZEN SKINHEADS THAT TURNED INTO ASSHOLES, AND ALL OF THEM ENDED UP GETTING THEIR HEADS KICKED IN." — MADDOG

"THE SKINHEAD BATTLE? STUPIDITY AND IGNORANCE FUELLED IT FOR YEARS." — B. BOB

+++

162

THE GLOBE AND MAIL
APRIL 9, 1988

CHONG-SU LEE, OWNER OF LEE'S PALACE ON BLOOR STREET WEST, SAID HE STOPPED BRINGING A POPULAR PUNK BAND CALLED BFG TO HIS CLUB BECAUSE IT ALSO ATTRACTED SKINHEADS, WHO FOUGHT WITH THE PUNKS AND VANDALIZED NEIGHBOURING STORES.

SKINHEAD VIOLENCE BEGAN WITH THE SOCCER HOOLIGANISM IN BRITAIN IN THE 1950'S. THE WEAPONS THEN WERE SHARPENED COMBS. TORONTO POLICE SAY ALL THOSE ARRESTED RECENTLY WERE ARMED WITH KNIVES.

MANY OF THE SKINS ARE ON WELFARE AND BEG MONEY FROM PASSERSBY. DRUGS, LIKE ACID AND GLUE FOR SNIFFING, WHICH IS CHEAP AND EASILY OBTAINED, ARE WIDE-SPREAD AMONG THE SKINS WHO LIVE ON THE STREET.

+++

"WE WERE TRYING FOR IT NOT TO BECOME A WAR. ONE THING LED TO ANOTHER AND IT ALL ESCALATED. YOU KNOW BIFF STARTED THE WHOLE THING. THEN HE GOT DANGO INTO IT. THEN A BUNCH OF THE OTHER SKINS GOT INTO IT. THEN IT BECAME A SKIN VERSUS PUNK THING. THEN ONCE WE BEAT THOSE GUYS UP, IT BECAME A REVENGE THING. WE'D BEEN IN A BAND FOR ABOUT THREE OR FOUR WEEKS, WHEN THIRTEEN GUYS WITH 'REVENGE' WRITTEN ON THE BACKS OF THEIR HANDS BROKE INTO OUR HOUSE WHEN WE WERE PLAYING AT THE UPPER LIP. IT WAS PRETTY FLATTERING." — CRAZY STEVE GOOF

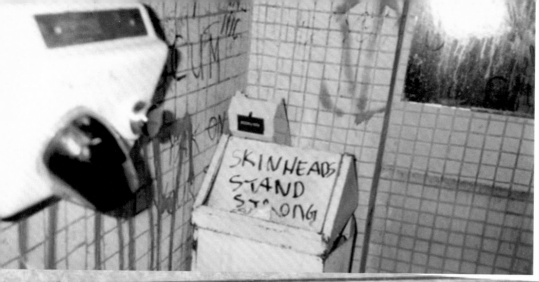

**JOCKO THOMAS
reports from
police headquarters**

teens clubbed with crowbars
n west-end punker gang fight

Two young men were bludgeoned with crowbars in a fight between
val punk-rock gangs in Toronto's west end.

Jason Ford, 17, of College St. is in Doctors Hospital with serious head
juries and Scott Wiebe, 19, of Kitchener has a broken arm and leg in-
ries.

The fight broke out early Sunday when four men smashed their way
to a College St. home near Brunswick Ave. wielding crowbars. Police
id the incident was reprisal for an earlier pitched battle between be-
veen rival groups at College St. and Augusta Ave.

Scott Fenimore Shropshire, 27, of Sullivan St. faces two counts of
ggravated assault and weapons charges, including careless storage of a
rearm.

"THERE WAS AN INCIDENT IN WHICH SOME PUNK SCUMBAG WAS OVER AT THE HEAD NAZI'S HOUSE, BIFF'S, AND STOLE SOMETHING, I THINK IT WAS A STAMP COLLECTION OR WHATEVER. HE DIDN'T DO IT BUT A BUNCH OF SKINHEADS SHOWED UP AT THE FORT. THEN LATER A BUNCH OF PEOPLE FROM THE FORT WALKED INTO BIFF'S HOUSE AND PRETTY MUCH BEAT THE SHIT OUT OF HIM." — MADDOG

"[THE GOOFS] CAME LOOKING FOR ME AND BIFF ONE NIGHT, WHEN WE USED TO LIVE OVER TOP OF THE FREE TIMES CAFÉ. BUT BIFF AND I WEREN'T THERE – WE'D MET A COUPLE OF WOMEN AND WE WERE HANGING OUT WITH THEM ALL WEEKEND. AND THESE GUYS CAME IN AND THEY KICKED THE SHIT OUT OF THE GUYS THAT WERE STAYING AT OUR PLACE; TWO GUYS WHO JUST HAPPENED TO BE OVER AT OUR PLACE THE NIGHT THEY CAME OVER AND THEY GOT SMOKED. THEY HAD CHAINS, BATS, FRYING PANS . . . APPARENTLY IT WAS VERY BAD. THAT SHIT WAS INTENDED FOR ME AND BIFF, FOR SURE." — BRUNO

"I REMEMBER ONE NIGHT WHEN THAT WHOLE THING WAS GOING ON WITH THE SKINS AFTER DANNY GOT HIT IN THE HEAD WITH THE FRYING PAN, THEY HAD BLOCKED THE DOOR TO THE FORT, AND ALL THEY LEFT WAS THE LITTLE FLAP FOR THE DOGS TO GO IN AND OUT. SO PEOPLE HAD TO CRAWL THROUGH THAT LITTLE HOLE. I'M THERE TRYING TO FIGURE OUT, GEE DO I GO OUT SIDEWAYS, DO I SQUEEZE OUT THIS WAY OR THAT WAY . . . FORWARD OR BACKWARD . . . IT WAS SUCH A MINDFUCK FIGURING OUT HOW TO GET THROUGH . . . BUT I MADE IT." — SEWAGE

"IT WAS A FORM OF GANG WARFARE THAT WAS GOING ON. ABSOLUTELY. WE WERE SKINHEADS, WE FEARED NOBODY. ESPECIALLY IF WE WERE WALKING AROUND IN A GROUP OF FOUR OR FIVE." —BRUNO

"THE SKINHEADS SHOWED UP ONE TIME TO POUR GASOLINE DOWN THE TOP OF THE FORT TO BURN THEM OUT." — B-BOB

"AT THAT TIME, SKINS WERE A KIND OF PANDEMIC. THERE WERE A LOT OF THEM. WHEN THEY SHOWED UP THEY KIND OF POISONED THE SCENE, WHICH IS WHY YOU WANTED TO KEEP THEM OUT. ONE THING ABOUT THE SCENE AROUND THE GOOFS WAS THAT IT WAS KIND OF HEDONISTIC. THEY WANTED TO HAVE THEIR OWN BAR, THEY WANTED TO HANG OUT, THEY WANTED TO LISTEN TO MUSIC, THEY WANTED TO DRINK AND RIDE THEIR BIKES AND EAT SPICY SHRIMP ALL DAY IN THE SUN. IT WAS A PRETTY LAID-BACK SCENE, WHEREAS THERE WAS NOTHING LAID-BACK ABOUT SKINHEADS. IT'S REALLY FUNNY BECAUSE, MUSICALLY, IN A LOT OF WAYS, THERE'S NOT MUCH DIFFERENCE." — RICK McGINNIS

+++

NOW MAGAZINE
FEB 23-MARCH 2, 1988

SKINS EXPRESS THEIR PATRIOTISM BY OPPOSING NON-WHITE IMMIGRATION AND ENGAGING IN "QUEER BASHING." ASSAULTING GAY PEOPLE, WHOM THEY CONSIDER PER-VERTED, IS ONE WAY FOR YOUNG SKINHEADS TO GET THEIR FIRST TASTE OF BLOOD.

TERRITORIAL GANGS INCLUDE THE DOWNTOWN OR YONGE AND ISABELLA SKINS, THE EGLINTON SKINS AND THE WEBBS OR THE WEST END BOOT BOYS AND THE SCARBOROUGH SKINS.

LIKE ANY ARMY, SKINS HAVE A UNIFORM, WHICH IS DISTINCT. A SKIN IN FULL BATTLE UNIFORM WILL MOST OFTEN HAVE A SHAVED HEAD AND MULTIPLE TATTOOS, AND USUALLY WEAR DOC MARTENS BOOTS, A BLACK BOMBER JACKET AND ROLLED UP JEANS, SUSPENDERS AND, DEPENDING ON HIS MOOD, A CANE.

ONE GROUP THAT HAS HAD RUN-INS WITH THE SKINS OVER THE YEARS IS THE PUNK BAND BUNCHOFUCKINGOOFS.

OUR SITUATION ISN'T ONE OF 'SKINS' AND 'GOOFS,' IT'S ONE OF 'GOOFS' AND ASSHOLES," SAYS STEVE JOHNSON, LEAD SINGER FOR THE BUNCHOFUCKINGOOFS. ACCORDING TO JOHNSON, DURING A RECENT GIG IN KITCHENER, A SKINHEAD IN THE AUDIENCE WAS SNIPING AT THE BAND DURING THE PERFORMANCE, WITH A 22-CALIBRE PELLET GUN."

+++

"THE SAME GROUP OF SKINHEAD GUYS WOULD COME ROUND THE FORT ONCE OR TWICE A YEAR, USUALLY ON A SUNDAY. THEY'D GET THERE EARLY IN THE AFTERNOON AND START BUYING BEERS AND APOLOGIZING FOR THE LAST TIME THEY WERE THERE. THE GOOFS WOULD START LOOKING AT EACH OTHER AND SMILING, BECAUSE THEY KNEW WHAT WAS GOING TO HAPPEN. THE SKINHEADS WOULD GET HAMMERED, START SOME SHIT, TRY TO BE TOUGH ABOUT IT, GET TOTALLY BEATEN UP AND LEAVE. THEN THEY'D COME BACK IN SIX MONTHS AND DO IT ALL OVER AGAIN...STARTING OUT WITH THE APOLOGIES, SAYING LET'S BE FRIENDS, GET MORE AND MORE DRUNK AND THE NEXT THING YOU KNOW, THERE'D BE A BIG FIGHT AGAIN."— MICUS

"ONE TIME MIKE SMALLSKI AND I FOUGHT AT THE GREEN P PARKING LOT IN KENSINGTON MARKET, RIGHT BESIDE THE FORT. HE SHOWED UP IN THIS BLACK NINJA OUTFIT WITH FOURTEEN-HOLE STEEL CAP BOOTS ON. I PUT ON MY BEST PANTS AND MY FRED PERRY, POLISHED MY BOOTS. CUT MY HAIR. RINGS ALL OVER MY FINGERS AND WEARING MY JACKET. THERE WAS PROBABLY SEVENTY OR EIGHTY PEOPLE SITTING ON THE ROOF OF THE FORT WATCHING. WE FOUGHT FOR FORTY-FIVE MINUTES. I WAS HANGING ON FOR DEAR LIFE, TRYING TO STICK MY FINGERS IN HIS EYES. HE WAS TRYING TO BITE MY FINGER OFF. HE ALMOST DID. WE WERE DEADLOCKED IN THE END." — BRUNO

+++

THE SATURDAY SUN
APRIL 2, 1988

IN DOWNTOWN TORONTO RECENTLY, A GANG OF SIX SKINHEADS – ALL MALE – BEAT A MAN DURING A ROBBERY, KICKING HIM AGAIN AND AGAIN WITH THEIR HEAVY DOC MARTENS BOOTS. THEN FOR NO APPARENT REASON, A CHELSEA, A FEMALE SKINHEAD, STEPPED IN AND STABBED THE VICTIM.

ON ANOTHER NIGHT, NOT FAR AWAY, A TEENAGED GIRL WAS VICIOUSLY SLASHED BY A MALE SKINHEAD.

THE GIRL WAS ABLE TO GET HER HANDS UP TO SHIELD HER FACE BUT SUFFERED LONG, DEEP CUTS ON BOTH ARMS FROM THE EXACTO KNIFE HER ATTACKER USED.

+++

"EVEN TO THIS DAY, THERE ARE NO SKINHEADS IN THE MARKET. I BET YOU, EVEN TWENTY YEARS FROM NOW, IT'S SOMETHING THAT A SKINHEAD FATHER TELLS THE SKINHEAD SON: 'DON'T GO TO THE MARKET, SON.'" — WILLIAM NEW

ol Saskatchewan

wan has introduced
A letter from Mr. ...
Mr. Devine, released yesterday,

LANGUAGE — Page A2   AIRLINER — Page A2   McDOUGALL — Page A2

Aimless violence sparks a police crackdown

Thirty skinheads were arrested last week, most on robbery, assault and weapons charges, said Constable Alex Poole of 52 Division, which covers the downtown area.

The arrests followed a rising number of armed street robberies by aimless groups of male and female skinheads who congregate at the Eaton Centre and in the alleys and arcades of Yonge Street between Queen and Bloor streets.

These gangs are preying also on other street children, Constable Poole said, although most such attacks go unreported.

Skinheads are concentrated in Toronto's downtown, along Yonge, Queen and Bloor streets, although police in Scarborough found a group living in the tunnels of Kennedy subway station several weeks ago.

Many are relatively peaceful and have a job and a place to live, but an aggressive minority live on the streets, sleeping in stairwells in cold weather.

Skinheads, known as skins, have sometimes drifted to Toronto after crackdowns by police in cities such as Montreal.

One youth who called himself a right-wing but

peaceful skinhead says the Toronto skins are very disorganized compared to those in the United States, where some belong to the Ku Klux Klan and fascist groups.

The skinhead, who moved to Toronto from Detroit last November, says he feels safer on Toronto's streets although he says he is often harassed by police and other gangs.

"But my friends from Detroit say it's crazy here because you've got skinheads fighting each other,"

POLICE — Page A10

Metro police step up patrols to counter skinhead violence

● From Page One

said the youth, who asked not to be identified.

The pack violence associated with a small core of skins makes even some police officers nervous. About two weeks ago, a skinhead gang surrounded a police cruiser parked near the Eaton Centre and began rocking the car.

Constable Poole and other officers worry that the recent problems reflect a growing boldness among the skins.

Skinheads have been involved in an ongoing cycle of violence and revenge between underground youth groups such as punkers —

devotees of punk music who often wear outlandish fashions and hairstyles — and preps, clean-cut teenagers who go to school and only hang around downtown on weekends.

Many officers fear that the street violence and retaliation by victimized groups could flare up into a serious problem this summer if police do not "nip the problem in the bud," Constable Poole said.

Police are especially concerned about a faction of skinheads known as "Nazis" who hold white supremacist views and have been blamed for seemingly purposeless and unprovoked violence.

Two weeks ago, a gang attacked two businessmen in the middle of the day for no apparent reason at the north end of the Eaton Centre. Centre security guards said one man's jaw was broken in three places.

In another recent attack, an 82-year-old Italian woman was beaten and kicked by a gang of six or seven skinheads, police said. Her house was ransacked but nothing was stolen.

Since the arrests last week, many skins have been staying out of sight and street kids who live around the Eaton Centre complain that they are being unfairly harassed.

Several punk teen-agers said the police and the public are exaggerating the problem of skinhead violence, although they agree that a small minority are dangerous, especially when in a pack. Still, they stress that most of the violence is turned inward as street groups fight each other.

Last Sunday night, for example, police had to quell a fight between a gang that included punks and skins and another group of teen-age skateboarders called Untouchables.

The fight began on the platform of the Yonge-Bloor subway station and spilled on to the tracks and through the subway tunnels, forcing the Toronto Transit Commmission to turn off the power at 1 a.m. for about 20 minutes.

Downtown club owners increasingly are banning skinheads from their premises in an effort to reduce the violence and vandalism.

Chong-Su Lee, owner of Lee's Palace on Bloor Street West, said he stopped bringing a popular punk band called BFG to his club because it also attracted skinheads, who fought with the punks and vandalized neighboring stores.

The Twilight Zone, a downtown late-night dance club, stopped regu-

X-PLODING GLUEBAGS

U STICKY FACES NOW INVADE THE SCENE
DEGENERATE GLUEHEADS - U THINK U'RE MEAN
HUFFING THAT CRAP MAKE U FEEL TOUGH - THE
CHIPS ON YOUR FACE SHOW U'VE DONE ENOUGH
THAT SHIT ROTS YOUR BODY AND THEN YOUR MIND
2 KEEP ON GOING U'D HAVE 2 B BLIND - THE
REEK OF YOUR BREATH IS GETTING VERY STALE
3 DAYS LATER IT STILL TELLS THE TALE
THE BAG ON YOUR FACE - THE DROOL ON YOUR
CHIN - "HEY WHERE'S MY LAST TUBE" - U JUST
CAN'T WIN - A HUFF AND A PUFF AND WE'LL
KICK YOUR FACE IN - I KNEW THIS SONG WOULDN'T
GET THRU - SO I'LL TELL U WHAT I'M GONNA
DO - I'VE GOT MY BIC - RITE HERE IN MY HAND
COS DEATH'S THE ONLY THING U UNDERSTAND
CRUCIFIED BY COMBUSTIBE FUMES - MY LIGHER SPELLS
EXPLODING DOOM - DESTROY U WITH THE SHIT
U INHALE - ILL US MY BIC INSTEAD OF NAILS
DOWN - DOWN - DOWN - DOWN - DOWN - DOWN - DOWN
EXPLODING GLUEBAGS IS SO MUCH FUN - DOMINION
DAY FIREWORKS INSTEAD OF A GUN - EXPLODING
GLUEBAGS IS SO MUCH FUN - QUIT THAT SHIT
NOW OR U BETTER FUCKING RUN - DOWN .

LYRICS - CRAZY

Bad Dream In Toronto

Harris and Lastman awoke together
Remembering the same dream
In three short years from now
Toronto's streets will be clean

With no more doorway panners
And not a single sewergrate drunk
With no more dirty squeegees
And no more street punks

Welfare will be gone and there'll be
No clients for the foodbanks
Children's Aid can play mommy
When single moms join jail's ranks

Then the city will be their
World-class whitewashed playground
And the tourists won't even notice
That there's no locals left around

With no more graffiti
And every doorway daily bleached
All the streets lit brightly
So visitors fears are out of reach
Then big business can boast
Of the best standard of living in the world
And bring in more cash for them
And give the poor what they deserve
Nothing

With the same mentality
Of a speeder when he's cleaning his house
There's no need to stop now
All the corner scum is on the way out
And quickly they saw that if they
Forced most of the poor to the curb
The police could collect the garbage
As their mission to protect and serve

With cutbacks and workfare
The sick and fucked are pushed to the street
Now at nite the parks are settled
Til the coppers walk their beat
Flushed from only a tree's shelter
And jackbooted out of doorways
Leaves only them with no options
So it's off to jail where they'll stay

But the jails were too crowded
So they'll build a megajail or maybe three
And promise to close the old ones
When all the cells are all free
But after the classist cleanup
They'll be pushed for more space
So all the jails will stay open
Packed with defectors from society's race

The next time they arose
After a nite of sucking each other's cocks
They perfected the ultimate plan
For making this town perfect for jocks
They sent out their goon squads
To crush vendors' fruit stands
And teach those sixty-year-old women
To shake the taxman's hand

The hookers and drug dealers
Were all easy pickings
And anyone who looked different
Got a good shitkicking
The media was bought out
Cos they all had corporate jobs
The system was making bucks now
Cashing in on new laws

Then they swept away the buskers
And stole all their lifesavings, change
They'll all join the robbers and rapists
When it's their new home on the range
Soon it will be pen time
For selling sunglasses without a permit
And now that it's started
There'll be no end to their shit

In many ways it's just the same as Hitler's dream
It's just how you view the streets as clean
If it were any one group but the indifferent
Racism or sexism would be your next rant
Some people don't want to play your games
You're sure that that's wrong that we all want the same
You should just leave it alone
Cos when it all gets real fucked
It'll be you that's to blame
That you're next out of fucking luck

Destroy All Automobiles

All the stupid jerks in their Eldorados
All those Rosedale pricks in their Silver Shadows
All those macho wops in their dingo-balled Trans Ams
All those hickey turds in their big wheeled Dodge Rams

Different types of status for different types of jerks
Living for their luxury cars with jerky vinyl roofs
Posing on the highways and posing in the street
Checking in the store windows
To make sure their hair looks neat

Destroy all automobiles
Destroy all cars
Attack 'em with Magic Markers
Crush 'em with metal bars

All those rocker buttfuckers
In their tacky plastic 'vettes
Looking for blond beauty queens
To keep as passenger pets

All those jocky faggots
In their customized cars at night
Cruise the street, they yell at us
Act like they want to fight.
No, they don't, they're very safe
As they drive away real quick
No parts at all to stop their cars
I wish they'd suck my prick

They wake up in the morning
And surely want to cry
Phone the pigs, the insurance man
Act like they don't know why

Well destroy all automobiles,
Destroy all cars
Destroy destroy destroy
Destroy, destroy it all

TORONTO

VOTE FOR CRAZY STEVE GOOF

THE POLITICS OF BEING A GOOF

IT'S NOT ENOUGH TO BE PUNK…
YOU GOTTA DO SOMETHING ABOUT IT

CRAZY STEVE GOOF got into politics because he hated the cops. Like other parts of his life, and in some ways like the history of the band, there wasn't a plan. Rather, bad timing on a bike was what forced Steve into action.

One night in 1985, on his way to play a Punk show at the DMZ, the cops stopped him. He wasn't doing anything wrong, he was just a Punk rocker, on a bike, at night, and that was reason enough for the cops.

By the time he got to the DMZ, he was late for his show and he was angry. He barked to the crowd that night that while the cops were questioning him, he told them, "One day you jerk-offs will be working for me. I'm going to run for mayor and I'll make you all jump in the lake." And so a politician was born.

Crazy Steve Goof's friend, and Citizen Greg's brother, Mark Harrington, had worked with the Libertarian party as well as a group of Anarchists called "The Unparty." Their political goals involved getting seats and dissolving them. Crazy Steve Goof and Mark started talking politics, and when Mark suggested he run for Alderman. Steve agreed, and Mark became his campaign manager.

Running for Alderman in the 1985 civic elections meant he could campaign in Ward 6, an area of the city that was one of the most ethnically, socially and economically diverse. More important, it included Kensington Market.

City Hall wouldn't let Steve run under the name of Crazy Steve Goof, even though the law states that candidates can run under the name they're known by in the community. Steve B.F.G. Johnson ran using the slogan, "It's Your Turn to Put a Goof in Government." Harrington got Steve into all-candidates debates where, despite a rough, sarcastic delivery style, he won people over.

Crazy Steve Goof was twenty-seven, and the youngest person on the ballot. On November 11th, the *Toronto Star* ran a double-page spread featuring every candidate running in the civic elections. Next to a photo of Crazy Steve Goof glaring into the camera was the following: "Punk Rock Singer wants the sale of certain glues banned as a measure against glue sniffing. The Ward 6 resident advocates closing Kensington Market to non-commercial traffic, Sunday shopping and increasing foot patrol policing in the downtown core."

Crazy Steve Goof had the support of folks in the Market. The owner of Café la Gaffe on Kensington Avenue made thousands of fortune cookies with "Vote for Steve BFG Johnson" on the inside and delivered them to restaurants all over Chinatown. "That was like the Market coming back to say thanks," says Scumbag.

Crazy Steve Goof spent a total of $190 on his campaign, and he did it without a telephone. Despite his few resources, 1,057 people put an 'X' next to his name on the ballot; that was 8% of the vote. It was one of the highest results ever for an independent in Ward 6. He beat out the Rhino, Libertarian and Communist party candidates, in fact, every party except the major three: Conservatives, Liberals and NDP.

Fast-forward three years . . . On October 26th, 1988 the *Ryersonian* newspaper ran a photo of Crazy Steve Goof on the front page. In it, he's walking down a street in Kensington Market, a cigarette in his mouth, wearing a rat-eaten shirt underneath a frayed, patch-laden army vest and looking like he just woke up from a three-day bender. Above the photo ran the caption: Would you vote for this man?

Despite the optics, he was serious about running again. This time around his slogan was, "Use your right to vote, or lose your right to complain." He was running in the same ward as before, now renamed Ward 5. His goal wasn't necessarily to win, but to get people to vote, especially ones who'd never voted before. Crazy Steve Goof knew only 25% of eligible voters had cast their ballots the last time he campaigned in 1985.

He told the Ryersonian, "If I got the seventy-five per cent of the people who didn't vote to vote, I would win by a landslide."

The interview was done in the Market, on a Sunday morning after Crazy Steve Goof had been up all night on acid. He told the reporter he had a beer under his coat. She described him as looking more like someone waiting for a rumble than a candidate for Alderman. He definitely wasn't just another pretty face, as the caption below the photo on the front page of the *Ryersonian* suggested.

"Last time I presented myself with a beer in my hand, in a leather jacket, unshaven for five days, looking up and telling someone not to bother me from a table in a bar," said Crazy Steve Goof. "This time, I will present myself in a similar manner."

Everyone at the Fort pitched in. The Punk factory switched from printing band flyers and t-shirts to handbills and 'How to Vote' pamphlets. They printed their slogan on small flyers and shoved them into those old cash envelopes tellers used to give out at the bank. They wrote money amounts on the outside of the envelopes and dropped them in different places around Ward 5: in phone booths, at bus stops, on the street, everywhere. It was guerrilla-style campaigning, before anyone came up with the term.

THE PROPAGANDA MACHINE

Already masters at printing band flyers, making the switch to political ones was easy for the Goofs. They had the machines, the paper (salvaged from a pile of junk that took up a whole floor above the Fort) and the Punk person power to do it.

One flyer read: "Dead Bored." It made a joke out of being a junkie, with lines like: "Heroin! 45 million dead junkies can't be wrong! Available now from a rich, well-fed murderer or a dying addict near you!"

The Goofs knew how to get their message across efficiently. Instead of wasting a whole page with one message, they put twelve of them on a sheet. That way 100 sheets of paper turned into 1200 flyers. Over 100,000 copies of "Dead Bored" were printed and scattered throughout the downtown core.

They'd leave them underneath pop cans left on the street, staple-gun them to old wooden telephone poles, drop them in phone booths, leave them in parks, in places they drank, on window ledges and wedged into every nook and cranny within biking distance of the Fort.

JUST SAY NO [TO SOME] DRUGS [RULE #5]

Drugs were part of the scene. Heroin, coke, glue, uppers, downers, pharmaceuticals and the list goes on. The Goofs weren't choirboys, they did the drugs until, like a lot of folks, they realized drugs were stupid, boring and could kill them, and so they stopped. Like former smokers who come to hate other smokers, the Goofs started to take a serious stance against hard drugs, especially cocaine, heroin and glue.

For them, drugs and being addicted to them was playing into the system. Being hooked meant

Photo in newspaper by Jeremy Gilbert

Member of the Ontario Community Newspapers Association

WEI

M
a
t

B.

Ry

to
in
Oa
ch
ye
se

to
Sa

co
St
vi
st
"
st
lis

sh
ha
m

Would you vote
For this man?

r,

gram is taking

student Chad
reed. "I know
and what I'm
ralize."
lso expressed
campus. He said
ts and faculty a
a high school.
embarrassed by
lding that he
with a member
community at
her than let him
ilding.
e his comments

e his comments
survey of 100

S

Punker run_s

'He's a
pleasant
alternative
to municipal

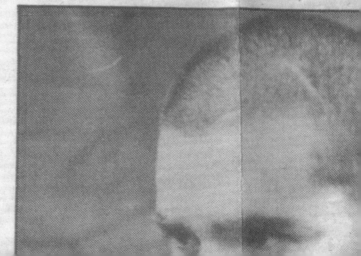

VOTE
STEVE B.F.G. JOHNSTON

Use Your Right to Vote, or Lose Your Right to Complain!

E HOUSING SHORTAGE IS'NT A PROBLEM
T SHOULD BE SOLVED WITH CITY BUILT
TTOS. IT IS A PROBLEM THAT COULD BE
EDIETLY RESOLVED BY GETTING RID OF
CITY BY-LAW THAT PROHIBITS
DENCES IN COMMERCIALLY OR
USTRIALLY ZONED AREAS.
S BY-LAW WAS INTRODUCED TO KEEP
USTRY FROM INTERFERING WITH THE
TS OF PEOPLE LIVING IN A RESIDENT-
AREA. A VERY GOOD IDEA FOR PEOPLE
DO NOT WANT TO LIVE NEXT TO A
TORY BUT TO THOSE WHO DON'T CARE
HOSE WHO HAVE NO FEASIBLE ALT-
ATIVE THIS COULD BE THE ANSWER
IDES, NO ONE SHOULD BE FORCED TO
IN THE DOORWAY OF A VACANT.
TED WAREHOUSE.

NOT ALLOWING A SMALL BUSSINESSMAN TO LIVE IN HIS WORKING ESTABLISHMENT THE CITY
RCING MANY OF THEM OUT OF BUSSINESS BY;
1. PAYING DOUBLE OVERHEAD WITH TWO RENTS.
2. PAYING TO COMMUTE.
3. WASTING TIME COMMUTING.
TIME MEANS MONEY

EEMS THE ONLY REASON THAT BITTERS WERE TAKEN OFF THE SHELVES WAS THAT THE
O. WERE NOT MAKING THIER CUT. WHY AFTER ALL THESE YEARS IS GLUE, ONE OF THE
APEST AND MOST DESTRUCTIVE HIGHS THERE IS STILL AVAILABLE TO YOUR CHILDREN ON
SHELVES OF YOUR CORNER STORE?

PROPOSED SPADINA LIGHT RAPID TRANSIT LINE WILL CREATE A PHYSICAL BARRIER DOWN
INA. PHYSICAL BARRIERS GHETTOIZE NEIGHBORHOODS AND OBVIOUSLY HAVE A VERY BAD
CT ON TRAFFIC.
ADINA SUBWAY LINE IS A MUCH BETTER ALTERNATIVE TO MEET THE NEEDS OF COMMUTERS
OUT INFRINGING ON THE RIGHTS OF THE NEIGHBORHOOD, OR WORSENING THE ALREADY
SPADINA PARKING SITUATION.
YOU THINK OF A BETTER WAY TO FORCE METRO TO REPAVE SPADINA FOR THE FIRST TIME IN
THAN A DECADE?

BY THE WAY, HOW'S YOUR WATER PRESSURE?

USE YOUR RIGHT TO VOTE OR
LOSE YOUR RIGHT TO COMPLAIN!
THIS TIME VOTE
E B.F.G. JOHNSTON 924-3347 for alderman in Ward 5

U HAVE NOT BEEN ENUMERATED FOR THE NOVEMBER 14TH MUNICIPAL ELECTION, GO TO THE POLL IN YOUR
ITH I.D. AND YOU CAN SWEAR AN OATH TO BECOME ELIGIBLE TO VOTE. YOU MUST BE A CANADIAN CITIZEN
YEARS OF AGE

for office

His main concern for this election is the proposed Light Rapid Transit for Spadina Ave. He says the LRT will create a physical barrier on Spadina, cutting the market off from the rest of the area. Left-hand turns will be more difficult, and police assistance between divisions 52 and 14 will be hampered.

Metro too cheap

being under someone else's thumb. You were in debt — literally and figuratively to "the man" and for Punk rockers, this wasn't cool. So they cleaned themselves up, still kept smoking pot, made beer their vice of choice and took a hard line against hard drugs.

"We got a lot of people off drugs," says Crazy Steve Goof. "That's one thing the band truly helped change in a whole bunch of people's lives...stopping them from becoming total drug addicts."

"They were the first crowd I met in the hardcore scene that were anti-drug," says Citizen Greg. "To me, 'Punk' meant drug addict. I was an intravenous drug addict addicted to coke, speed anything that would get me up. When I showed up in '85 at the Fort, Micus and I really got into this 'No Need For Needles' campaign. And I just decided nothing goes in my arm except something administered by an M.D."

"When I moved into the Fort, I was whacked on acid," says Micus. "I was doing so much acid that I couldn't really live anywhere else. I quit school, then I started selling acid. At one point I was doing five hits a day. I did eighteen in one day and didn't really get high and realized, okay, I'm saturated."

Crazy Steve Goof says he would make a terrible crackhead. For him, beer was a better, slower death compared to sticking a needle in your arm.

"I know exactly what drugs are about because at some point or another, I did all of them," says Crazy Steve Goof. "There's a psychological thing where it stops being about the drug and it's about the feeling of the fuckin' needle freely moving through the wall of your vein and not touching any of the sides. Like people who shoot pharmaceuticals that they don't even get high on. They just want to punch holes in themselves."

It was around this time that crack started hitting the streets. The new drug was cheap, easy to find and superaddictive. The Goofs became hardcore, anti-coke crusaders. "Coke: The Real Thing For Real Assholes" says it all:

So you've put yourself on Death Row
It's where you want to be
You're wasting your life doing blow

Fuck, I'm glad it's you not me

You look like death warmed over
Wrinkled old and pale
Every spike that stabs your arm
May as well be a coffin nail

"One of the fuckin' funniest things I ever fuckin' did right, was I saw an advertisement for the Addiction Research Foundation...they wanted to talk to people who'd quit doing coke and crack without going on a program," says Crazy Steve Goof. "This little geeky doctor guy asks me how I quit doing coke. And I told him it was really simple...I went out and made a bunch of buttons that said Coke, The Real Thing For Real Assholes. Then I put one on. And then I put on a show in the park in front of my whole community. And then every time somebody said the word 'coke' to me, I just punched the shit out of them. And he's like, 'you're joking.' And I'm like, 'well actually, no.' I go, 'If you want to offer me blow, I'm going to treat that as you're threatening my life, and I'm going to act accordingly.'

That concert, in the summer of 1989, was part of a cocaine awareness day. Micus came up with the "No Go for Blow, Bro!" slogan, even painting it on his leather jacket. Proclaiming, "The Snowstorm is Melting," the BFGs held a concert in Bellevue Square Park. Armed and Hammered also performed that day, along with a couple of reggae bands. A local MPP gave a speech, as did an AIDS awareness group. There was also a comedy show, a theatre troop and clowns.

Previous page, bottom right: 7:06 is Crazy Steve Goof's way of saying 666 [666 minutes = 7 hours and 6 minutes.]

Previous spread, top right: Crazy Steve Goof and Citizen Greg celebrating after being given an award by the Kensington Market Residents' Association for helping reduce crime and drugs in the 'hood. The award was a free dinner at Planet Kensington. Wine included.

SPECIAL
VOTE BxFxGx
SPECIAL
VOTE BxFxGx
SPECIAL
VOTE BxFx6
SPECIAL
VOTE BxFxG
SPECIAL
VOTE BxFxGx
SPECIAL
VOTE

So you've put yourself on death row
It's where you want to be
You're wasting your life doing blow
Fuck, I'm glad it's you not me
You look like death warmed over
Wrinkled old and pale
Every spike that stabs your arm
May as well be a coffin nail
Well you're so fucking cool
Cos you live so fucking fast
The odds are in favour
You just won't fucking last
Coke is crap, you know it's shit
A fucking waste of time
You're just an asshole mixing hits
Or snorting up that line
Playing baseball's even worse
The fastest deathrace thru town
At five bucks a freebase toke
You look like a fucking clown
Coke is crap, the real thing
Classic shit for classic fools
Well you're a classic asshole
Cos you think it fucking rules
You buy your broads with blow
A few lines are worth a fuck
But when your snowstorm melts
You'll be out of fucking luck
You say you don't put out cash
To get your pecker wet
Bread or blow it doesn't matter
Whores are all you get
You've burned all of your friends
And owe all over town
Just to ride the terror train
To fall, sorry I mean come down
Coke is real you poor lost souls
Coke's the real thing for real assholes
Real assholes just like you

SON, CRAZY STEVE BxFxGx 7:06
& DIRT
TO: MIKI TOMA
ON "COKE THE REAL THING~FOR REAL FOOLS LIKE
ESS: 253 COLLEGE ST
BOX 313
TORONTO ONT M5T 1R5

FILM

CRAZY STEVE GOOF AND THE GOOFS HAVE APPEARED IN 140 TV SHOWS, MOVIES AND A COUPLE OF STAGE PLAYS. MOSTLY THEY "PLAYED" BAD GUYS. MOSTLY THEY PLAYED THEMSELVES. NO WARDROBE REQUIRED.

Amerika.Part.1.of.5.avi

Crazy Steve Goof was riding his 1930s bicycle through Kensington Market early one morning. He was wearing a fedora and long overcoat. Dirt was hooked to his chain belt, carrying an enormous, bleeding cow leg that weighed so much his head was bobbing. Crazy Steve Goof saw a craft services truck, stopped and grabbed a coffee and was asked if he wanted to be in a film. All they wanted him to do was be himself and ride down the street again with Dirt. Sadly, the scene ended up on the cutting room floor of David Cronenberg's The Fly.

Using prop guns in a performance of Macbeth, the actors were afraid the Goofs had real guns at home and would bring them to the theatre and accidentally shoot someone on stage. Instead, the director made everyone go "Bang, Bang," with their fingers.

+++

Crazy Steve Goof got to chase Mr. T down a staircase with a wooden pole in an episode of the television show T. and T. Crazy Steve Goof's favourite part of the job was gorging himself on craft services food, while the crew, amused and afraid of Dirt, fed him endless amounts of filet mignon and broiled swordfish.

+++

They always played the bad guys lurking in the background, the ones getting arrested or the ubiquitous Prisoner #2, on the TV show, Night Heat. On one shoot at the now-closed Mimico Lunatic Asylum [yeah, that's what it was actually called], they spent their time off set skateboarding in the tunnels and trying to break into padded cells to smoke pot. One time, Crazy Steve Goof played a Nazi Skinhead wearing a Hitler t-shirt and a swastika on his forehead.

+++

Cast as . . . you guessed it . . . punks on Street Legal.

+++

Played a group of futuristic transsexual cross-dressers called The Scavengers on War of the Worlds.

+++

One scene in Alfred Hitchcock Presents had them pulling up in a car, jumping out, grabbing a brick, smashing a pawn shop window, grabbing an amulet, diving back in the front seat of the car through the window and speeding away. They did it in one take and got a standing applause from the crew.

THE TWIN DRAGONS
MICHAEL & MARTIN
McNAMARA

DRAGON HUNT
THE ULTIMATE SURVIVAL GAME

CINEPLEX ODEON THEATRES

VIDEO
STREET DATE
February 28, 1991

Crazy Steve Goof played a narc on Katts and Dog.

+++

The Internet Movie Database voted Twin Dragon Encounter and its sequel Dragon Hunt the worst movies ever made. In them, Crazy Steve Goof plays henchman to B-Bob's villain. The movies were mostly written on the spot. Crazy Steve Goof's role mostly just involved him punctuating everything B-Bob said by cocking a sawed-off shotgun and smiling. B-Bob forced the director to shoot all his scenes before noon, before he and Crazy Steve Goof got too smashed

At one point, the twin stars of the movie, Michael and Martin McNamara told the students in their kung fu club not to fuck around with the Goofs, saying, "You guys think you can fight, but these guys will kill you." After accepting an invite to come for a beer in the Market, the twins arrived in the middle of a fight between the Goofs and a bunch of guys they didn't know. The kung fu experts got to witness the Goofs throwing a wrench through the back window of the "bad guys'" car.

+++

Millennium was an implausible movie about a guy investigating a fatal airplane crash who discovers an organization of time travellers from a polluted Earth, out to seek revenge on those who caused the crash and resurrect the dead. The movie stars Kris Kristofferson and Cheryl Ladd. After casting him, the casting director asked Crazy Steve Goof to help find extras because they needed a lot of people with shaved heads to play futuristic alien types. This meant they had to hire Skinheads, because in those days you couldn't pay squares to shave their heads. Crazy Steve Goof did some of recruiting from Evergreen, a youth drop-in centre on Yonge Street. The only thing Crazy Steve Goof had to agree to was that he wouldn't beat up the Skinhead extras on set.

+++

Freakshow was a low-budget horror anthology about two teens who visit a cut-rate carnival sideshow. The Goofs were playing dead people in graveyard when Goof Terry Rubberstone did some mushrooms and passed out covered in sticky goo and dirt. He woke up in a graveyard, freaking out and screaming, "Who did this to me?" Dirt the dog lost his canine mind and spent the whole time howling and digging at graves. Thor was buried alive, given a rubber hose to breathe through and promptly forgotten about. It was only after his arm shot up through the earth — like a zombie from Michael Jackson's Thriller video — that anyone remembered he was there. All that happened on one day. Oh, and one extra detail...the head makeup guy was pissed off at Crazy Steve Goof for spending all his time trying to screw the makeup girl.

+++

It all ended for Crazy Steve Goof in 2000, when he showed up on set and the director looked at him and said, "We can't use this guy, he's too old to play the leader of a youth gang." His agent told him if he grew his hair, she could get him lots of roles playing cops. He passed.

THE BFGs AND
THE BERLIN WALL

KIERAN PLUNKETT GOES TO BERLIN, EVADES THE STASI
AND LAUNCHES THE GOOFS INTO INFAMY

"I SPRAY-PAINTED the Bunchofuckingoofs' name onto the Berlin Wall in the summer of 1989, two months before it came down. Stasi [East German state security service] stationed in watchtowers were looking down at me and filming me as I did it. The six metres of wall I painted was actually on East German soil, so my graffiti crime was indeed committed against the East German government.

"My girlfriend Laura and I had been refused entry when we tried visiting East Berlin through Checkpoint Charlie a few days before. They told us we were 'not suitable' enough to visit the DDR. My hair was dyed green and yellow; Laura's was pink and green. So the next day we bleached our hair, Laura covered hers with a scarf, this time we dressed more conservatively and they let us in.

"We knew the wall was going to come down so we wanted to put our mark on it. When we returned back to London, everything came to a head; the border was thrown open. The East German government resigned and thousands flocked to the west in November of 1989."

— *Kieran Plunkett*

+ + +

The piece of the wall with the Goofs' name on it was part of a sale by auction in June of 1990 called *Le Mur de Berlin – Vente aux Enchères à Monte Carlo*, and later exhibited as part of The Berlin Wall in Basel in June of 2007 during Art Basel.

The photograph on page 186 was taken during an exhibition in front of the Elisabethenkirche, a church in the heart of Basel, Switzerland. The pieces of the wall in the picture belong to two guys from Basel who bought them in the auction in Monaco in 1990. The pieces are in storage at a warehouse in Basel. They're in mint condition...and for sale.

How to Dress Like a Goof

Seeing a bunch of them at once, especially with their dogs, scared the crap out a lot of people and that was the point. They wore their weapons -- chain belts with seatbelt buckle clips and spiked bracelets, black, steel-toe army boots worn in the freezing cold and boiling sun. Artfully torn t-shirts riveted together with safety pins and staples; topped off by a personalized leather jacket. Kensington Market was the perfect place to find everything from old pajamas and worn ballet tutus to used army pants and other stuff people didn't want. They had to be able to run, fight and fuck without too much of a hassle.

"THE ANARCHY PUNKS WHO LIVED UPSTAIRS DESIGNED ARMOUR SUITS FOR US. PEOPLE WOULD COMPARE US TO COMIC BOOK HEROES."
— CRAZY STEVE GOOF

"OUR CLOTHES AND OUR MAKEUP WERE A PROTECTIVE SHELL. IT WAS A CREATIVE THING TO SHOW OFF YOUR INDEPENDENCE. BUT, IT WAS ALSO A MASK THAT PROTECTED YOU FROM A WORLD THAT SCARED YOU, SO YOU TRIED TO SCARE THE WORLD BACK." — COLLEEN SUBASIC

"BACK THEN YOU WERE PUTTING YOURSELF ON THE LINE. YOU WERE MAKING A STATEMENT ABOUT SOCIETY." — MIKE SMALLSKI

"IT WAS UNTHINKABLE TO LOOK PUNK. I GOT SPAT ON IN THE STREETS AND THREATENED ON THE SUBWAY. THE TORONTO OF THE LATE 70s, EARLY 80s WAS A LOT MORE VIOLENT. I USED TO SEE DRAG QUEENS GETTING CHASED DOWN THE STREET AT YONGE AND WELLESLEY — AN AREA THAT'S NOW A GREEN ZONE FOR GAYS. IF YOU LOOKED PUNK, YOU COULDN'T HOLD DOWN ANYTHING LIKE A NORMAL JOB, WHEREAS THAT'S NOT THE CASE ANYMORE." — RICK McGINNIS

"RANDOM JOCKS WOULD YELL AT ME ON THE STREET: 'YOU'RE A FUCKING FREAK! I'M GOING TO KILL YOU!' YOU KNOW HOW MANY FUCKING FIGHTS I GOT IN OVER THAT?"
— CRAZY STEVE GOOF

#190.

TIPS & TRICKS FOR DRESSING LIKE A GOOF

#1.
DON'T BUY IT, MAKE IT. [RULE #5]

#2.
FISHING LINE OR DENTAL FLOSS WORKS BETTER THAN THREAD.

#3.
LIQUID PAPER IS PERFECT FOR WRITING ON LEATHER JACKETS.

#4.
BUY YOUR ACCESSORIES AT THE LOCAL HARDWARE STORE.
HOSE CLAMPS MAKE SNAPPY FINGER RINGS AND FOR BRACELETS,
TRY RUBBER DRAIN STOPPERS.

#5.
TRANSITION FROM WINTER TO SUMMER BY CUTTING THE FINGERS OFF
YOUR GLOVES AND THE SLEEVES OFF YOUR JACKETS AND SHIRTS.

#6.
GET A TATTOO, PAY FOR IT WITH BEER.

#7.
SILKSCREEN YOUR OWN T-SHIRTS — BAND LOGOS PREFERRED.
THESE CAN ALSO BE SOLD FOR CASH.

#8.
SEW POCKETS INTO EVERYTHING. THAT WAY YOU CAN CARRY BEER,
BAND FLYERS, DOG TREATS AND STUFF YOU DON'T WANT TO COPS
OR BOUNCERS TO FIND.

#9.
LAYER EVERYTHING, THEN MARINATE YOURSELF IN ALCOHOL
SO YOU WON'T FEEL THE COLD.

#10.
TREAT EVERYDAY LIKE IT'S HALLOWEEN.

THE TORONTO SUN

THURSDAY, JULY 23, 1998   104 PAGES   50 CENTS

MAYOR:
IT'S WAR
ON SQUEEGEES

"I USED TO DO FAKE BLACK EYES ALL THE TIME. NO ONE COULD EVER GIVE ME ONE."
— CRAZY STEVE GOOF

~~DA BFG CEE~~

~~WARS FOR A TERRITORY~~
~~WARS FOR A SPACE~~
~~WARS FOR THE GROUND YOU STAND ON~~
~~WARS AT YOUR PLACE~~

~~WARS WITH THE PROJECT BOYS~~
~~AND WARS WITH THE SKINS~~
~~WARS WITH THE LOCAL MOB~~
~~ALMOST WARS WITHIN~~

~~WARS AS A WAY OF LIFE~~
~~WARS THAT MAKE NO SENSE~~
~~KILLING ON YOUR OWN DOORSTEP IS~~
~~YOUR ONLY LEGAL DEFENCE~~

~~WARRING'S NOTHING NEW TO US~~
~~PEACE IS OUT OF PLACE~~
~~DON'T BRING YOUR SHIT UPON US~~
~~OR WE'LL BE STOMPING ON YOUR FACE~~

~~EVERY DAY'S A BATTLE~~
~~THE ASSHOLES NEVER STOP~~
~~JERKS PUSHING FROM ALL SIDES~~
~~IT'S FUN TO WATCH 'EM DROP~~

~~WE NEVER INSTIGATE IT~~
~~OR BRING IT UPON OURSELVES~~
~~IT SEEMS OUR LIFESTYLE'S A MAGNET~~
~~FOR PEOPLE WITH POOR MENTAL HEALTH~~

~~IT'S NOT A REFLECTION OF OUR TRIP~~
~~COS WE'RE NOT FOOLS~~
~~IT SEEMS THAT EVERY FACTION~~
~~HAS A DIFFERENT SET OF RULES~~

~~YOU KNOW IT'S NOT A REFLECTION~~
~~OF OUR TRIP COS WE'RE NOT FOOLS~~
~~YOU KNOW THAT EVERY FACTION~~
~~HAS A DIFFERENT SET OF RULES~~
~~HOGS OF WAR~~

~~EVERY ROAD'S THE 401~~
~~SIX LANES FOR YOU TO EVERY CAR'S ONE~~
~~DON'T STOP FOR SHIT, DON'T HESITATE~~
~~TURN OUT OF IT   NEVER BRAKE~~
~~TRAFFIC LAWS WERE MADE FOR CARS~~
~~THOSE ASSHOLES DRIVE WITH NO REGARD~~
~~SHOW NO RESPECT FOR YOUR LIFE~~
~~PUSH YOU OFF THE ROAD TO IMPRESS THE WIFE~~
~~THEY HAVE MORE CASH AND PAY MORE TAX~~
~~THEY OWN THE ROAD   NOT MAD MAX~~
~~THEY WANT A WAR~~
~~THAT'S WHAT THEY GET~~
~~WE'VE GOT MORE RIGHTS~~
~~THAT'S WHAT THEY FORGET~~

~~LET'S START A WAR   IT'S TIME TO FITE~~

~~LET'S START A WAR IT'S TIME TO FITE~~
~~CHASE 'EM, CATCH' EM AT THE LITES~~
~~STEEL TOES MAKE COSTLY DENTS~~
~~HE'LL PAY DOLLARS NOT JUST CENTS~~
~~YOU CUT ME OFF YOU FUCKING WHORE~~
~~I'LL CRASH YOUR CAR   I'LL CRUSH YOUR DOOR~~
~~PLASTIC CARS ARE SUCH A SCORE~~
~~I'LL DO IT NOW AND I'VE DONE IT BEFORE~~
~~FUCKING CARS THEY PUSH THEIR WEIGHT~~
~~STUCK IN TRAFFIC HAVE TO WAIT~~

195

~~CRUSH YOU   KILL YOU TO GAIN AN INCH~~
~~RUN THE REDS AND RISK THE PINCH~~

~~BIKE ANIMALS   WE DRIVE TO KILL~~
~~RIDE HARD AS HELL   AND NEVER SPILL~~
~~HOGS OF WAR   ARE THE BETTER WAY~~
~~YOU DRIVE FREE   YOU DRIVE FREE AND MAKE THEM~~
~~PAY~~

~~YOU'RE SO   STUPID   I MIGHT BE DEAD~~
~~DOWN ON THE ROAD WITH A CRACK IN MY HEAD~~
~~YOUR FIRST CONCERN'S INSURANCE RATES~~
~~I'VE GOT NO RIGHTS   I'VE GOT NO LICENSE PLATES~~
~~I'LL BLOW YOUR MIND AND FUCK YOUR DAY~~
~~GET ON MY BIKE AND BUZZ AWAY~~
~~THE DAMAGE THAT'S BEEN DONE~~
~~HAS BEEN DONE TO YOU~~
~~THE REPAIR BILL IN YOUR HAND~~
~~IS WHAT REALLY HURTS YOU~~
~~ANY FUCKING ASSHOLE~~
~~WITH EVEN HALF A BRAIN~~
~~KNOWS THAT EVERY VEHICLE~~
~~IS GUARANTEED A FUCKING LANE~~

TITLE: KING KONG & LITTLE SUSIE
SUBTITLE: SOME THINGS ARE JUST MEANT TO BE

King Kong believed it was his destiny to be in the Bunchofuckingoofs.

He left home as a teenager. Family problems. He describes his dad as a crazy alcoholic, says one of his brothers "sucked off a shotgun" and his mother lost her mind. He moved to Cobourg, Ontario, and lived in a tent. Not long after that he jumped on a bus and headed to Vancouver, figuring once he got out there, he could collect welfare. But his mother soon put a stop to that.

"Mom decided to fuck up everything for me and told welfare to send me home," says King Kong. "She wanted the support payments."

While he was in Vancouver, he decided he wanted to be in a band, even though he couldn't play an instrument or sing. He bought a Dead Kennedys album and got on the Fringe Records mailing list. That's how he heard about the Goofs.

Before he left Vancouver, he bought the cheapest "piece of shit" bass he could find by trading in a Game Boy, and used his first and only welfare cheque to buy a 5257 Czech assault rifle. He bought the gun legally.

He put the bass in a pillowcase and the gun in a guitar case and locked it up with a piece of chain. Then he bought black market prescription codeine to stay whacked out for the five-day bus ride home. He made a dozen meat and cheese subs to last the ride, but they got stolen along with a bag of Allsorts Nibs.

On the bus, some crazy old guy was telling a creepy, scary story when — right at the climax — an owl flies into the front window of the bus, smashing it open. While waiting for a new bus at a layover, another passenger saw his bass and asked if he was in a band. "Yeah, I am," King Kong said. "The Bunchofuckingoofs."

He didn't know how to play the bass when he bought it, but figured it would be easy to learn because you only play one string at a time.

Seven years later, he was living in Oshawa, playing in bands and working at the Million Dollar Saloon strip club as a bouncer. A perfect job for a six-foot-eight, 450-pound, bald-headed dude. He'd just left his wife and six-year-old daughter.

In 1997 King Kong heard that Shitloads of Fuck All needed a bass player. He went to the audition but ended up playing for the Goofs, replacing Godzilla. They had one rehearsal before they played their first show together.

Fast-forward two years. Little Susie, five-foot-three and 110 pounds was at Punkfest. She was married, worked in IT and was at the park in Marmora with her brother. It was there she heard a story about "the biggest guy you've ever seen," named King Kong, running naked through the bush.

Five months later, she's hanging with her brother at the Duke of Connaught, when in walked "the biggest guy she's ever seen." He went over to say hi to her brother and knocked over Little Susie's beer. She pretended to be irate so he bought her another one. Thanks to a lack of chairs, she ended up on his lap. Before last call, King Kong said to her. "You better go now, before I take you into the bathroom and fuck you." It was a huge turn-on for a straight-assed IT girl.

Little Susie was twenty-four and had never seen a live show in a bar. King Kong gave her a flyer for a Goofs show at the El Mocambo with Vice Squad and Shitloads of Fuck All. It was King Kong's birthday. She went to the show and it changed her life. She left her husband and young son and started dating King Kong.

At first, she couldn't listen to the Goofs' music. But then, she says, she got hooked on the lifestyle, the chaos and the craziness. She was the total opposite of the people she was now living with.

A couple of years later, Little Susie and King Kong were still together, when King Kong's other brother killed himself, also with a shotgun. It was Remembrance Day, 1999. Superdepressed, he quit the band only to re-join in 2001, just before their second cross-Canada tour. His brother's last request was that half his ashes be spread in the Pacific, the other half in the Atlantic. King Kong and Little Susie drove the ashes out west. He describes the trip as being like a funeral march.

Little Susie drove the tour bus taking him and the band on tour across the country. "It's an extreme sport, driving a van for a Punk rock band," says Little Susie. She drove from Toronto to British Columbia and back. Seventeen shows in twenty-one days. She was paid five bucks a day.

King Kong called playing with the Goofs, "a rolling comedy show." This tour was no exception. He had worked in film and stage production for years and brought that element to their live shows.

King Kong shared the Goofs hate-on for cops. For one of his characters, he dressed up like a cop, topped off with a giant pig's head that he made. He pumped the head full of fake blood using an air-compressor. On tour, the band would start the show throwing donuts at the crowd. Then Crazy Steve Goof would shoot King Kong Kop with a fake 9mm gun, pretending to blow his brains out while fake blood spewed onto everything and everyone. He also liked to rev up a chainsaw during shows and slice the tops off beer bottles with it.

The Goofs always carried half-used bottles of anti-crab shampoo with them. When they got pulled over by the cops, who would inevitably search the van, the Goofs made sure the bottles were in plain sight. They would all start scratching themselves. The search would end fast. There were no pat-downs.

King Kong also liked to clown around…literally. He dressed as Fisty the Clown, a classic clown look: big red nose, extra large lips and frizzy, synthetic wigs. He'd wear leather vests on top of his clown suits. The whole get-up was more scary then funny. He wasn't going to any kids' parties.

On that second tour, King Kong thought he saw a couple of UFOs in the sky over Saskatchewan. He saved a girl from her boyfriend during a fight in Sudbury, which ended with him getting stitches in his forehead and the boyfriend's ear almost being severed by a broken beer bottle. In Kingston, they got into a huge brawl with forty or fifty people, on a fairground right across from the Civic Centre. Driving through the Rockies, they came across an overturned Kraft cheese truck and loaded up with a thousand dollars worth of plastic-wrapped, processed cheese slices. They were sealed together, like sausage strings, and King Kong wrapped them around his chest, Rambo-style, and ate them as he drove the van.

Little Susie and King Kong are married and have kids together.

ON   TOU R

BUNCHOFUCKINGOOFS CANADIAN TOUR 1991
SUGGESTED KIT LIST

ITEM	MAKE	BORROW	FIND	BUY	YES	NO
BAND ACCESSORIES ~~SNARE~~						
TOOL KIT						
PROPS:						
– BARS						
– SAWS						
– STAND COLUMN						
– AXE						
–						
–						
~~DRUMMER ACCOMODATION~~						
2 X 100' EXTENSION CORDS						
2 X 15' " "						
PISS BUCKET						
DOG BOWLS						
DOG FOOD						
" " CONTAINER						
~~LAUNDRY POWDER~~						
VEHICLE EQUIPMENT:						
–BOOSTER CABLES						
–WIND SHIELD WASH						
–SNOW CHAINS						
–OIL						
–ICE SCRAPER						
2 X TIRE INFLATOR						
–2 X PADLOCKS(1 KEY X2)						
–4' CHAIN						
–ELETRIC HEATER						
–ROAD MAPS						
~~PAPER TOWELS~~						
2 X GAFFER TAPE						
4 X WHITE						

(handwritten margin notes)

KILO 20
BASS 15
DROMS $80

KIND — AXE
AH —
PISS BUCKET / DOG FOOD

AC —
Drs —
P
O.
Rags —
Knife —
~~More~~
Pm —

F Longs

merchande – badges
– shirts
Tapes – 10mm
– Boomo Kit

pils 12
Italo SUSSANA

SECURITY

REMEMBER: EVERYONE IS GOING TO VANCOUVER. WE HAVE NO BACK-UP
IF SHIT HAPPENS. ANY ASSHOLE WITH A BEEF WILL USE THIS
OPPORTUNITY TO GET ONE OF US. ASSUME EVERYONE OUT THERE HAS
A GUN AND WANTS TO USE IT ''''''

1. The door will have a key in/key out or panic bar system.
   Use it at ALL times
2. Slide bolt to be used only after all residents are in.
3. If you are out late, call first so you are expected and to
   check if any shit has gone on while you were out
4. No one stays over unless you know them VERY well and they
   know about how this place runs. - we don't need some moron
   leaving without getting the door locked after them!!
5. Answer the door with caution - check completly before you
   open it. Even if the person claims to be Steve's "oldest"
   friend, if you don't know them, they don't get in. If you
   are unsure, tell them to call when Simon is in if it is
   important
6. ANSWER ALL PHONE CALLS' It could be important
7. IF YOU ARE IN TROUBLE, LEAN ON BELL. SOMEONE WILL BE THERE
   WITH A BASEBALL BAT ETC.

THE PHONE

1. Answer the phone politly. Use only " B A " no stupid shit
   like "Back Alley Bar & Grill". Most of us will be trying
   to get jobs. DON'T BLOW IT''
2. ANSWER ALL PHONE CALLS. It could be Steve calling on tour
   or one of us in shit. Also movie calls can come at wierd
   hours - they are worth big bucks
3. The answering machine will be turned on every night to get
   messages form Steve. It will be set to 10 rings so try
   and get it first.
4. All important calls go to Simon

MONEY

1. Pay all future etc. rent money as soon as you get it!' We
   need back-up cash for bills etc. Pay CASH to Simon
2. TURN ALL LIGHTS OFF WHEN NOT IN USE, INCLUDING LOFTS'''

NOISE/PARTIES

1. No parties during the working week : Sun-Thur
2. During the week, ALL noise (music etc.) stops at 11 pm
3. NO parties on the weekends (No Greeks crowd etc)
4. Only CLOSE friends to come over, only after you have talked
   to the rest of the house first

F: HOUSE JOBS

1. Back from Lisa's room to be vapour-locked
2. Back to be painted
3. Garbage under loading dock to be thrown
4. Bike pile to be moved under loading dock
5. Lock to be put on green fridge, we all get keys
6. New slide bolt - LISA & TERRY TO BUY NEW LOCK
7. Shit in front of paint room to be moved to back after paint
8. New paint on toilet and shower floor

MAJOR CLEAN-UP ON SUNDAY : BE THERE !!!!

1. Clean all your mess as soon as you are done
2. Kitchen and bathroom get extra treatment. Clean your
   dishes, don't leave them around
3. Clean hair out of shower, flush dirty water down the drain
   with jug and brush
4. Small garbage out on Monday
   Big garbabe out on Wednesday
5. Nothing goes down floor drains (beer, dog piss etc.)
6. Put dirty dishes in a sealed bucket in room if you don't
   want to wash them right-away
7. Use ashtrays at all times. We will try to get metal cans
   with sand in them

ART CEASER 688 6851 STACY #181 Seymour
BOOZE (AN)
CLUB SODA
PUMP

2

D) The driver and one security person shall be made in time for the gig.

wrap the merchandising while the second security person
stays with the band.

10) A cymbal case shall be made in time for the gig.

11) All illegal and otherwise props shall be stored
and locked in the black road box and strictly for use on
stage.

12) GIG SHEDULE:

Date	City	Venue	Amount	
04/01/91	Toronto	Rivoli	$400.00	(our door)
12/01/91	Winnipeg	Mc Blah	$350.00	+f+ac+ex
16/01/91	Regina	Student Union	$450.00+80%+950	Svc Sr. 265 5x
		Brent Caron		
		(306)584-7600		
17/01/91	Saskatoon	Skatepark	$300.00	266
??/??/??	Edmonton	???	???	
19/01/91	Calgary	Westward Club	$350.00 +f+ac+ex	
24/01/91	N/Van	Carl	$250.00	+f+ac+ex 461
		(604)980-2240		
25/01/91	Van	Cruelele	$300.00	80% door WTFHAK
??/??/??	Vic	(604)688-8748		

GIG CASH TO DATE $2300.00
BEER TOTAL TO DATE $0950.00

CASH TO DATE $3250.00

214 E14 MURRAY
386 0240

****

1

Dear Goofs and "road-crew",
                             Since our conversation p.m
03/01/91 we have concluded the following and this
discussion make all previous discussions null and voi

1) We do not want to take a "winnabago".

2) We want to take a "van" and make horisontal
adjustments for KIRK.

3) The persons who are travelling with the band
follows:5 X GOOFS
        1 X DRIVER
        2 X SECURITY
        1 X SOUND/MERCHANDISING PERSON

Total= 9 Persons

4) Since we are headlining each and every gig th
merchandising shall commence from the moment we arriv
the gig thru until the equipment is loaded onto the
van(i.e. the last thing on the truck is the merchandi

5) Per Diems shall be issued to each person ($20
and they shall, on a personal level function by thems

6) No person at anytime leave the de-bussing poi
without telling at least two other crew members where
going,who he is going with and for what reason.

7) There are NONE WHAT SO EVER IN THE WAY OF AFT
ACTIVITIES.(We do not pay bail or ambulance charges u
a third party is at fault!)

8) Dogs shall remain on chains,unless in the bus
being supervised by their OWNERS!!!!!!!!!!!!!!!!!!!!!!
They shall remain in the band room (on chains with wa
and food) and be walked regularly.

9) Since we are headlining at the end of the gig
shall happen:A) The on stage security shall remain on
once the band has left the stage.
          B) Once the band decides to return to th
stage they shall wrap their equipment the stage secur
shall stay on the stage until this has been completed
          C) When this has been done and EVERYTHIN
been accounted for KIRK shall stay with the equipment
the entire crew (less the merchandiser) loads the
equipment.

M E17
MURRAY
386 0240

```
GIG CASH TO DATE    $2300.00
BEER TOTAL TO DATE  $0950.00

CASH TO DATE        $3250.00
```

****

<u>FACTS AND FIGURES</u>

OAC

1614.50.

1)Mini-bus for 3 weeks=$~~1811.25~~   *no comfort
                                           *lots of piss stops
                                           *lots of food stops
                                           *same gas

2)Winnabago for 3 weeks=$1863.00   *loads of comfort
                                           *no piss stops
                                           *no food stops
                                           *same gas

W4 SSR

30 ACWG 300
1 FD
2 Regina 450 .
3 WINN   350
5 T BAY   200

595 R

BETTY GIRLFRIEND
CEDAR HILL REL CENTER
GARY BRANLESS
383 883

3 GUYS
386 0240

PHOTO: MIKI TOMA

ALCHOHOLIDAY TURNED ALCHOHOLOCAUST —

STARTED OUT AS RECREATIONAL, NOW IT'S GETTING QUITE HABITUAL
ONE WAY OR ANOTHER ITS MEDICINAL, ALCHOHOLIDAY TURNED ALCHOHOLOCAUST
ALCHOHOLIDAY TURNED WAKING UP IN A SEA OF CRUSHED TALL BOYS OF X
ALCHO HOLIDAY TURNED WHAT A GREAT FUCKING HANGOVER, ALCHOHOLIDAY
NOW ABOUT A BREAKFAST BEER, COME ON i NEED ONE, ALCHOHOLOCAUST TURNED x4
        OH WHAT A LAUGH, HA! HA! x2
WHATS A 6 PACK, i DON'T KNOW, BLACK RUSSIANS ROOL, BETTER THAN BLOW,
BANG DOWN A 2-4, LET THE PISS FLOW, OH WHAT A LAUGH, HA! HA! x2
BOOZING 4 BREAKFAST, THE WAY TO START, STRAIGHT ROCKET FUEL, LAST NITES BEER FART,
PUKE ON THE SIDEWALK, IT'S BLOOD AT LEAST PART

OH WHAT A LAUGH, HA! HA!
OH WHAT A LAUGH, HA! HA!
OH WHAT A LAUGH, HA! HA!

TOO BAD —

THE BRUISE ON YOUR ARM, GIVES U AWAY
SO U'LL BE A JUNKIE FOR THE REST OF YOUR DA
IT'S PART OF YOUR TRIP, STARDOM- COOLNESS & DEATH
THE NEEDLES THE WAY 2 INSTANT TOUGH,

YOU SHOULD DO BAD DRUGS, 2 BAD DRUGS DO U
YOUR WEAKNESS IS SHOWING, YOUR JUST ABOUT THROUG
                YOU'VE TRIED TO DESTROY AL
                BUT NOW U HAVE FAILED
                YOU'R NUMBER IS UP
                U'RE ABOUT 2 B NAIL

                    TOO BAD!!
                              °o°

ANOTHER WAR
THE NUCLEAR WAR
THE NUCLEAR WAR
THE NUCLEAR
WAR
OH, YEAH!

THE NU...

ALBUM ART

by John Groves

THE LAST SHOW

TO BE CONTINUED ...?

TWENTY-FIVE years to the day after their first show, the Bunchofuckingoofs played their last. No one knew it was going to be the last one: not the audience, not the band.

On November 26th 2008, the Bunchofuckingoofs played a show at Toronto's Kathedral. Crazy Steve Goof was on the mic, Katy was on bass, Fetus and Mike Murderio were on guitar and Goose was on drums. Those are the facts.

Everything other than that is a mystery wrapped inside a drunken Punk riddle. When it comes to what happened at the club that night, tongues have gone numb. No one will talk, not even anonymously.

Rumour has it there was pre-show consumption of mushrooms and acid, on-stage fist fighting, flying instruments, flying spit, a couple of nervous breakdowns and a trip to jail — actually that's a fact.

Fetus — who was born after the band – coughed out, "Whoever wasn't terrified, I am sure was entertained." That was all he would say.

If you have read the rest of the 224 pages of this book, it's hard to imagine what could have gone down that was so crazy and twisted that no one will talk about it.

Around this time, Crazy Steve Goof expounds, "The band became something it was never supposed to be . . . a band."

Crazy Steve Goof still has the booze can beer cooler, acid bunny and studded baseball bats. They're safely stored away along with the Goofs' twenty-five-year legacy.

DISCOGRAPHY

_ THERE'S NO SOLUTION, SO THERE'S NO PROBLEM (2 X 7") 8 SONGS (BACK ALLEY RECORDS) 1986

_ DRUNK, DESTROYED, DEMOLISHED (CASSETTE) 7 SONGS (BACK ALLEY RECORDS) 1989

_ CARNIVAL OF CHAOS AND CARNAGE (CD) 16 SONGS (FRINGE RECORDS) 1992

_ TOTALLY UNMARKETABLE (CD) 9 SONGS (BACK ALLEY RECORDS) 1997

_ BARRAGE OF BATTERY AND BRUTALITY (CD) 13 SONGS (GOD RECORDS) 2000

_ ASSAULTING AVERAGE ASSWIPES (CD) 11 SONGS (BACK ALLEY RECORDS) 2008

COMPILATIONS

_ QUESTIONABLE (12") 3 SONGS (JONESTOWN RECORDS) 1984

_ A TOUCH OF FRINGE (FRINGE RECORDS) 1993

_ DEAD ON THE ROAD — SONGS WITHOUT KEYBOARDS (RAW ENERGY RECORDS) 1993

_ DISEASE CONTROL – VOL. 1 (MUCK RECORDS) 1999

_ KIN OF KENSINGTON – GLOBAL SYNC MEDIA PRODUCTIONS 1999

_ THE INTERNATIONAL PUNK (10-CD BOX SET) 2001

_ CANUCK PUNK 2007

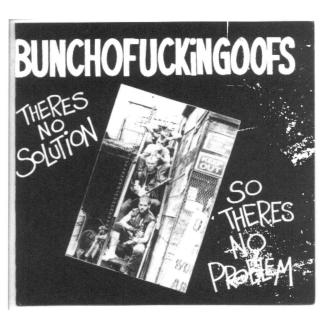

FOR A FULL DISCOGRAPHY INCLUDING LYRICS AND LINKS
GO TO WWW.DIRTYDRUNKANDPUNK.COM

nmarketable

Side One

1-CRACK ATTACK
2-LITTLE BROTHER WATCHES
BACK
3-GET A BIKE ASSHOLE
4-FACIST STATEMENT
5-HAVE YOU EVER SEEN

Side Two

1-TRUST ME
2-ALCOHOLIDAY TURNED
ALCOHOLOCAUST
3-HAVE A NICE LIFE
4-PROBLEM
5-KNOCK'EM'DOWN

UKINGOOFS

U FIRST
ECORD?

NO PROBLEM!
GOOFS 19.AD
HYPOCRITES SEX
SCO G.

ONES
YOU!)

PUNK ROCK IS AN ALLEYWAY WITH BROKEN GLASS, SYRINGES AND USED CONDOMS AND FUCKING DERELICT BROKEN WINDOWS . . . THAT'S PUNK ROCK. THE NEW STUFF IS ANNOYING."

— CRAZY STEVE GOOF

All living things have their colours
worn on their back
worn on their sleeves
expressed by instinct
declared in art
studded in struggle
painted in peace
dangled in wealth
embroidered in hope
bangled in humour
pinned in pride
displayed in sex
expressed by preference
shown in their style
shown in their eyes
All human beings have their say

From *Dressed to Kill* [1987] a book of poems
by Dawn Mourning

FOUNDING MEMBERS

1. **CRAZY STEVE GOOF** – vocals [Formerly bass for 4.5 Reasons For Retroactive Abortion, PolitiKILL inCOREct, B-Bob's Banned, Brutally Honest]

2. **BRIAN "SCRAG" GALLAGHER** aka By-T – bass [Presently bass for The Lower End]

3. **MADDOG** aka Kirk – drums [Formerly drummer of Fingerbanger, Blibber and the Rat Crushers]

4. **BAMBI** aka Jules – guitar [Formerly guitar for The Excretions]

PAST MEMBERS

5. **KATY** – bass [Formerly singer for Fucknuckles, bass for SLORC]

6. **GREGGOOSE** – drums [Presently drummer for Son Of Bronto, The Punching Nuns, formerly drummer for Brontocrushrock]

7. **FETUS** – lead guitar and back up vocals [Formerly lead guitar for Throwaways]

8. **MIKE MURDERIO** – rhythm guitar

9. **MERRICK "SCUMBAG" ATKINSON** – bass [Presently bass with Lummox and formerly bass with Fingerbanger]

10. **GODZILLA** – guitar [Formerly of Elvis Manson and Brass Knuckle Therapy]

11. **CISCO** – Dr. Valdez – vocals on "Religion Made By Hypocrites"

12. **THE TEPPERMAN BROTHERS** — vocals on "Sony Walkmans"

13. **T-BAG** – guitar

14. **BARON WASTELAND** – guitar [Formerly of 4.5 Reasons For Retroactive Abortion and Brutally Honest]

15. **JOHN "YNGWIE GROVESTIEN" GROVE** — bass and guitar [Formerly of almost every Punk band to ever exist in Toronto and presently AWOL]

16. **TERRY RUBBERSTONE** – guitar [Formerly of Grouphome]

17. **MIKE ANUS JAK** – guitar [Formerly of DayGlo Abortions, the Impaired and Karnig]

18. **THOR** – bass [Formerly of Armed and Hammered and Perdition]

19. **STOMPIN' AL MILLER** – guitar [Formerly of Living Proof and formerly of Fingerbanger]

20. **STEDS DEAD** – guitar

21. **HARDCORE DAVE** – guitar [Formerly of Armed and Hammered, Nun'oyerFuckinBizness, No ID, Land Fill]

22. **AIROCK** – guitar [Formerly of Shitloads of Fuck All and the 3Tards]

23. **KING KONG** – bass [Formerly of SnapperHead, Fucknuckles and The Terrorists, presently drummer with Bouncing Betties]

24. **BONES** – guitar and bass [Presently guitar for SLORC, Fucknuckles and drummer for Pallbearer]

25. **CITIZEN GREG** – vocals on "Double Punishment" [Formerly singer for 4.5 Reasons For Retroactive Abortion, PolitiKILL inCOREct]

Special thanks to photographer and constant fixture at the Oxford Fort, Miki Toma.
To see more of his work go to www.mikitoma.com

Miki and Crazy Steve Goof

Airock: aka Eric. BFG guitarist

Bambi: aka Jules. Original BFG guitarist, artist, first girl to live at Baldwin Fort

B. Bob: BFG, musician, father of Mini-Goof

Bones: BFG guitar and bass

Bruno: aka Bruno the Bruiser. Slam-dancer, Skinhead, West End Boot Boy

Burp: aka Vic. Lived at Oxford Fort, master of Bop, "55" guy

Christian Cannibal: Music booker for Newmarket Youth and Recreation Centre

Carson T. Foster: Music booker at the Rivoli

Cisco: aka Francisco Valdez, Dr. Valdez. Ex-cop from Uruguay, Doctor of Nothing, fire-eater,
        performed with the BFGs, wrote/sang "Religion Made by Hypocrites"

Citizen Greg: aka Greg Harrington. BFG, musician, lived part-time at Oxford Fort

Chris Walter: Writer, publisher. www.punkbooks.com

Colleen Subasic: Writer, playwright, BFG friend

Crazy Steve Goof: aka Johnny, Crazy, Steve BFG Johnson. Back Alley Boy, BFG singer, songwriter, ringleader, master of Dirt

Cretin: aka Murray Acton. Guitar/vocals for the DayGlo Abortions

Dallas Good: Fourteen-year-old Goof Friend, played covers of the BFGs in band Force of Habit

Dawn Mourning: Poet, vintage clothing aficionado, BFG friend

Drool: aka Drew. Lead singer of Random Killing, art student, lived at Oxford Fort, master of Sheba

Edward Mowbray: Producer/ director of films, *Not Dead Yet* and *Punk X*

Fetus: aka Adam. Last BFG guitar player, born after the band started

Filthy Sean: Back Alley Boy, BFG, founder of Back Alley Records, master of Kaos

Godzilla: aka God. Back Alley Boy, BFG guitarist, master of Mudd

Goose: aka Greggoose. BFG drummer

Greenie: aka Lisa Green. Goof girlfriend, lived at Baldwin Fort

Gymbo Jak: Singer, DayGlo Abortions

Jenny Snot: aka Jenny Blackbird. BFG friend

John Borra: Musician, music booker, sound guy at the El Mocambo

John Tard: BFG friend

Katy: aka al-Qaetor. BFG bassist

Kieran Plunkett: Artist, musician, spray-painted Bunchofuckingoofs band name onto the Berlin Wall

King Kong: aka Big Jamie, Fisty the Clown. BFG bassist, now married to Little Susie

Kurt Swinghammer: Singer-songwriter, Market local

Little Susie: Drove van on one of BFG's cross-Canada tours, BFG merch bitch, now married to King Kong

Lynn Crosbie: Writer, poet, BFG friend

MadDog: aka Kirk, Kirky. Back Alley Boy, original BFG drummer, builder of Forts, master of Autumn and Berlin, lived at Baldwin and Oxford Forts

Max Hutchinson: Writer

Micus: Back Alley Boy, BFG, lived at Baldwin Fort, artist, master of Rat

Mike Jak: BFG Guitar, lived at Baldwin Fort, former guitarist for the DayGlo Abortions

Mike Smallski: Slam-dancer, master of Asso and Bo

Mike Stead: aka Sted's Dead. BFG guitarist

Mopa Dean: Armed and Hammered singer, BFG friend, hung at Fort

Mucus: aka The James. Honorary BFG and honorary DayGlo after catching a steel bar in the face at the Siboney Club, master of Ralf

Ossie: Luis Coffee Shop guy [Kensington Market, corner of Baldwin and Augusta]

Rick McGinnis: Writer and photographer, Goof friend

Rob Ferraz: Writer for Exclaim! Magazine

Rosina: aka The Frygirl. Music booker for Kathedral and RT Concerts

Runt: aka Alex Currie. Artist, Lee's Palace muralist, painter of The Goofs Last Supper [pg. 220]

Scrag: Brian aka By-T. Original Back Alley Boy, original BFG bassist, lived at Baldwin Fort, master of Slag

Scumbag: aka Merrick. BFG bassist, moved into the Fort at fifteen, master of Buddy

Sewage: aka Susan Rizzo. BFG friend, Steve's prom date [110]

Steev Morgan: Filmmaker, art student, hung around Baldwin Fort [shot teardown film [pg. 48]

Stewart Black: BFG friend, author of Spunky Punkette, singer for Blibber and the Rat Crushers

Stewart Scriver: Owner of vintage store Courage My Love in Kensington Market

Stompin' Al Miller: BFG guitarist, hung around for two decades

Susana: Ex-girlfriend of Crazy Steve Goof, artist, painter of Dirt [pg. 94]

Tanya Cheex: aka Feelin' Shitty Barbie. Creator of Phlemzine, BFG friend, waitress, salesgirl, burlesque performer, dominatrix, Market local

TaraTaraTara: aka Tara Shelli Gallagher. Lived at Baldwin Fort with her cat Peanut, married [with children] to Scrag

Terry Grogan: BFG friend

Thor: Back Alley Boy, BFG guitarist, Victor Pitskull creator, tattoo artist, bouncer, lived at both Forts, master of Hammer

Vic Notorious: Back Alley Boy, BFG chronicler, doorman at the Turning Point

William New: Musician, music booker of Elvis Mondays

TO EVERYONE WHO DUG THROUGH BOXES, DUG UP THEIR PAST, THEIR PHOTOS AND THEIR MEMORIES, SPOKE FREELY AND FRANKLY, SHOWED THEIR SCARS, SPREAD THE WORD, SHARED A DRINK, A SMOKE, OR A TACO.

TO EVERYONE FOR ALL THE OFF-THE-RECORD STUFF THAT COULDN'T BE PRINTED, EDWARD MOWBRAY FOR GETTING OUT OF BED AT THE CAMERON HOUSE AND SHOOTING TWO FILMS ON THE TORONTO PUNK SCENE, TORONTO COPS FOR INSPIRATION, THE STAFF OF THE TORONTO WESTERN HOSPITAL EMERGENCY ROOM AND FRACTURE CLINIC, KICK-ASS PHOTOGRAPHER CHRIS BUCK WWW.CHRISBUCK.COM, KURT SWINGHAMMER FOR HIS SONG, UNCLE ANUS, UNCLE COSTA AND MOOSE FOR BLOWING FIRE IN DRAG, LYNN CROSBIE FOR BEING A WILD CHILD, AND BUZZ BURZA FOR BEING A WILD MAN, LOBLAWS FOR ALL THE SHOPPING CARTS, THE BOYS FROM RANDOM KILLING AND DAYGLO ABORTIONS, THE SCOTT MISSION FOR BOLOGNA SANDWICHES AND LIVER SOUP, SPIDER – FOUNDER OF PUNKFEST – FOR THE HEAVIEST SHOWS IN THE UNIVERSE, GARY TOP FOR BOOKING THE GOOFS AT THE CONCERT HALL WITH THE CRAMPS, GLEN JONES AND JONESTOWN RECORDS FOR RECORDING *QUESTIONABLE*, MARKETEER AND ARTIST CHRISTOPHE BONNIERE, BACK ALLEY BOYS PLAY-WRIGHT COLLEEN SUBASIC, CRAIG DANIELS AND FIONA SMYTHE, ROB FERRAZ, JEREMY GILBERT, ALI RIZA KUTLU, MOPA DEAN, KATY, TANYA CHEEX, AIROCK, CITIZEN GREG, LITTLE SUSIE, AND MADDOG FOR ALL THE WICKED PIX, LYNDA SPARKS FOR LOVIN' THE MUSIC AND DAVID SPARKES FOR LIVING IT, MING, TANG, MR. SMITH AND FREDDY, FOR LIVING THROUGH IT AND THE TWIN DRAGON KUNG FU BOYS FOR KICKIN' IT OLD SCHOOL, GEORGE, THE BIKE MECHANIC IN KENSINGTON MARKET, BEER STORES EVERYWHERE, BRIAN TAYLOR – THE GRAND OLD WIZARD OF TORONTO HARDCORE – AT ROTATE THIS, KIERAN PLUNKETT FOR PAINTING BUNCHOFUCKINGOOFS ONTO THE BERLIN WALL IN THE SUMMER OF 1989 AND THE EAST GERMAN STASI FOR TURNING A BLIND EYE, HARALD LACHNIT, ANDREW O1: AKA ANDREW OWEN, PHOTO STOOP PHOTOGRAPHER, DAVID WALDMAN: AKA KID WITH CAMERA, ALISON FOX FOR BEING IN THE SCENE, TAKING GREAT BLACK AND WHITE SHOTS OF THE BALDWIN FORT AND DEVELOPING THEM HERSELF, STEVEN PERRY FOR TAKING THE ONLY EXTERIOR SHOT OF THE OXFORD FORT, JOHN LONG AT LONG AND MCQUADE FOR LETTING THE GOOFS BUY AND RENT GEAR WITH UNLIMITED CREDIT, JOHNNY THE GREEK FOR LETTING PUNKS TAKE OVER THE GREEKS, GIVING THEM A PLACE TO MEET, PLAY MUSIC AND CALL HOME, FEEDING THEM GOOD FOOD WHEN THEY

COULDN'T PAY, SMILING AT THEIR BULLSHIT ANTICS, GIVING THEM JOBS AND LETTING THE DOGS HANG ON THE PATIO, RUNT AKA ALEX CURRIE FOR PICKING UP HIS MARKERS AND JOHN GROVE WHO TAUGHT RUNT HOW TO DRAW BY LETTING HIM COPY HIS CARTOONS, CHRISTIAN CANNIBAL FOR PUTTING THE NEWMARKET PUNK SCENE ON THE MAP, FILMMAKER BRUCE McDONALD, SINGER MOLLY JOHNSON FOR FINDING THE FIRST FORT, EXTRAS CASTING DIRECTOR NANCY HASTINGS, ERELLA 'VENT' GANON, THE GUY WHO INVENTED TWIST-OFF BEER CAPS, SO MADDOG DIDN'T HAVE TO LOSE ANY MORE MOLARS, ERIC AND THE NORTHERN VULTURES, BIG MICHEL AND DAN WEBSTER FOR UNLIMITED GOOD TIMES IN MONTREAL, BRENDAN CARON FOR ORGANIZING THE "NO GO FOR BLO" CONCERT AND BEING CRAZY STEVE GOOF'S CAMPAIGN MANAGER, TO ALL THE PEOPLE WHO VOTED PERIOD DURING THE ELECTION CAMPAIGN, EVERY BAND THE GOOFS EVERY PLAYED WITH, NIGEL FROM AUSTRALIA'S RULE 303 WHO WROTE A SONG CALLED BUNCHOFUCKINGOOFS, PAULA TIBERIUS, MICUS FOR SLEEPING ON HIS FACE LOOKING LIKE AN UPSIDE-DOWN ICE CREAM CONE AND SPRAYING HIS HEAD WITH ACRYLIC PAINT, ALL IN A QUEST TO ACHIEVE THE PERFECT MOHAWK. AND — WHILE WORKING AT THE TORONTO WESTERN HOSPITAL — FOR TAKING LEFTOVERS FROM DOCTOR'S LUNCHES AND BRINGING THEM BACK TO THE BALDWIN FORT, AND USING THE HOSPITAL'S MOPS AND INDUSTRIAL CLEANSERS TO CLEAN UP THE PLACE, THE GIRL IN CALGARY WHO STUCK THE BEER UP HER BOYFRIEND'S ASS [GREAT STORY PG. 131] AND TO THE TRAN-SCRIPT LADIES FOR TRANSCRIBING THAT STORY AND MANY OTHERS AND NOT CALLING THE COPS ON ANYONE, EXCLAIM! MAGAZINE, KEITH CARMAN, MARGO KIDDER FOR USING THE OXFORD FORT AS A LOCATION FOR A FILM, SCARY MARY AND MARIKA FOR LEAVING NO TRACE, NANCY DREWS, BIG ANTHONY, KRIS KRISTOFFERSON, DAMIAN FROM FUCKED UP, STUART, SETH AND PETER SCRIVER, TO ALL THE STORES IN KENSINGTON MARKET FOR FEEDING THE GOOFS WITHOUT KNOWING IT, AND TO ALL THE DRIVERS OF THE MEAT TRUCKS FOR SUP-PLYING UNLIMITED BONES TO THE DOGS. AND FINALLY, CHEERS TO ANYONE LEFT OFF THIS LIST WHO SHOULDN'T HAVE BEEN.

was
ad
d'
ubby

B.F.G.

BAD

DEATHWISH '87

AIR CONDITIONED

BUNCHOFUCKINGOOFS

+ PiG TUMBLER + NEGATiVE GAiN

iN dog we TRUST

SILVER DOLLAR

— BESiDE THE SCOTT MISSION —

SPADiNA & COLLEGE

TTC
ke ban

FRiDAY JULY 17th

BRiNG i.D.
— OR ELSE —

CHRISTINE'S A COUNTRY GAL

ONLY $3 WHAT A DEAL

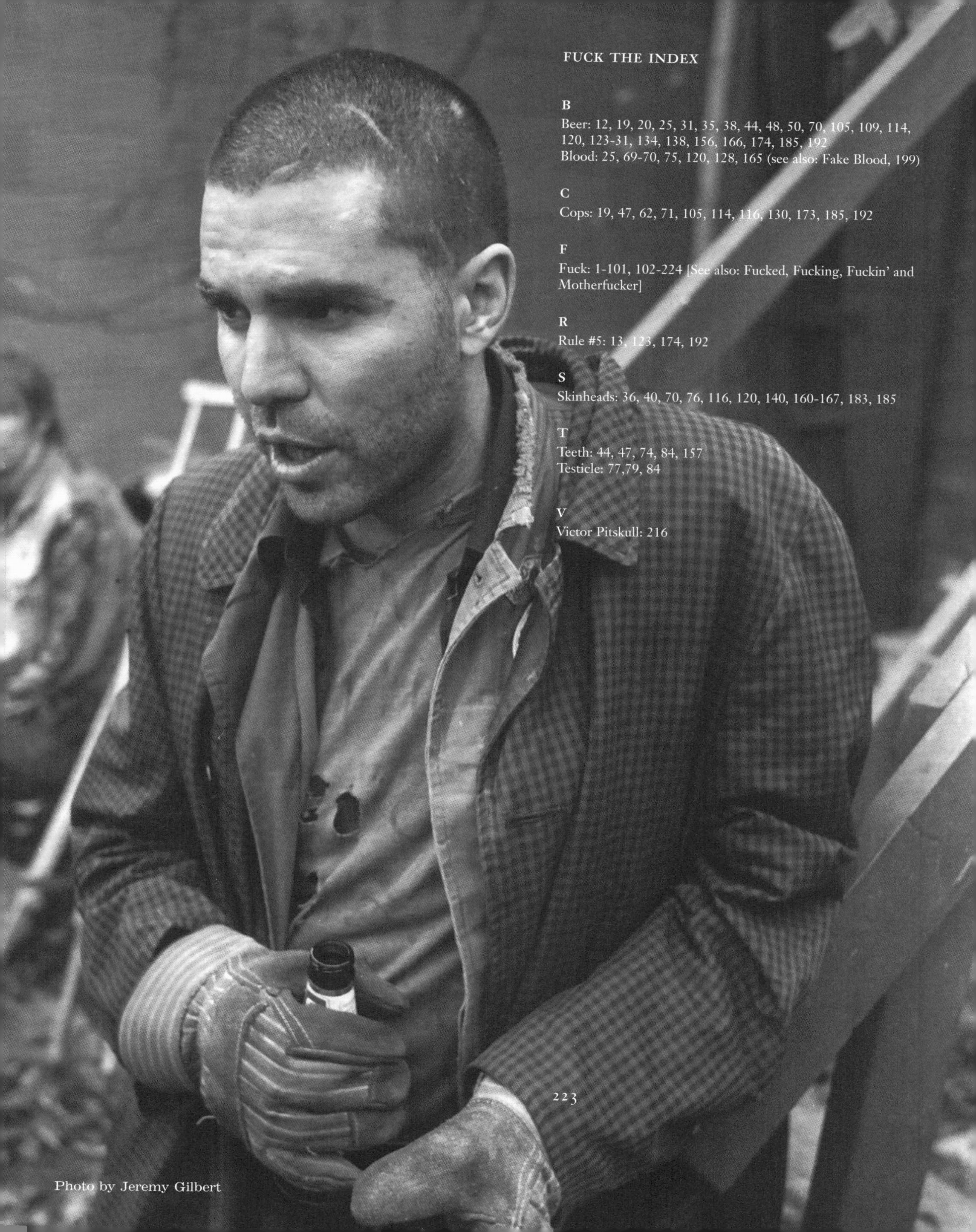

223

Photo by Jeremy Gilbert

And remember,
everything you heard
about us is true.
~ Crazy Steve Goof ~